# DELTA JACKS

## AND OTHER CARDS

# DELTA JACKS
## AND OTHER CARDS

J Whitley "Whit" Perry

Langdon Street Press

Langdon Street Press
212 3rd Avenue North, Suite 290
Minneapolis, MN 55401
612.455.2293
www.langdonstreetpress.com

ISBN - 978-1-934938-43-0
ISBN - 1-934938-43-2
LCCN - 2009920505

**Book sales for North America and international:**
Itasca Books, 3501 Highway 100 South, Suite 220
Minneapolis, MN 55416
Phone: 952.345.4488 (toll free 1.800.901.3480)
Fax: 952.920.0541; email to orders@itascabooks.com

Typeset by Madge Duffy

*Printed in the United States of America*

*On the cover*

The left cover photo is the original "Jack," who was named for a mule.
He started from scratch and acquired more than 17,000 acres during
the early development of the Mississippi Delta.

In the middle is his son, the irrepressible wild card of the deck, my daddy, Jack.

This is their story. Mine, too.
I'm on the right,
"Just Plain J,"
walking away.

# DEDICATION

*To all the "Queens,"*
*who tried their best*
*to keep all us knaves in line:*
*Miss Sallie, my grandmomma,*
*Momma,*
*Penny, my wife,*
*Ewee, the encourager, and*
*Bracie, "the Last of the Mohicans."*
*And to all my wonderful family,*
*especially Shiloh,*
*my gene pool.*

*Grandmomma*   *Momma*   *Penny*   *Ewee*   *Bracie*

*Shiloh*

# CONTENTS

# SPECIAL THANKS

I am deeply grateful to my wife, Penny, who has constantly encouraged me, daring me to become a better writer. An avid reader, she has offered invaluable insight.

This book would have been slow in coming if not for her and my old friend Jerry O'Roark, whose encouragement and keen observations have speeded the process. "Some folks may think that some of your stories are politically incorrect," Jerry says, "but they're the unvarnished truth."

Jerry has always been there for me. Years ago, when he was my boss and I was crippled by back surgery, he would drive me to and from the office and let me work while lying on a cot until I finally healed, over a period of months.

I'm thankful, too, for the photos and in-depth genealogical research that my brother George has shared. He is one persistent Perry! He and wife, Tina, have fourteen grandchildren, a veritable ocean of heirs.

Cousins Ouda Shellyn Pace Gresham, John Marshall, and Tina Gray have also shared their amazing research into both sides of my family tree.

Other cousins provided invaluable help, too. Jack Selman, the irrepressible "Bonehead," came through with a veritable treasure trove of old photos, and Jo Cochran helped out, as well. Brian Jacobs told me some great stories that I had forgotten. Robyn Dowdall chipped in with her eloquent poetry, Whitley Cox of Oklahoma shared some interesting lore, and Mari Messinger of Arizona came up with some great old Perry portraits.

Aunt Bracie offered some special memories.

Thanks, too, to friends Sterl and Cherie Owen of Tunica, Mississippi. They have always welcomed me with open arms, intellectual stimulation, and encouragement.

Author John Pritchard, a Tunica native, has been unbelievably supportive. He is a true gentleman and an amazing repository of knowledge.

Other Tunica folks pitched in, including attorney John Dulaney Jr., planter Edgar Hood Jr., and Dick Taylor, executive director of the Tunica Museum. Their help was invaluable.

And a special salute to Bill and Ann Petry, who have been like a second set of parents to me, first giving me a job as a spear-fishing instructor in the Caribbean when I was a teenager, and later encouraging me to start out on what would become an around-the-world odyssey.

Thanks, too, to graphics artist Jayme Ogles of LaGrange for her patience and assistance with the cover and photo layouts.

# MESSAGE IN A BOTTLE

This 1950's photo washed up in my email just before press time, with a message inscribed by Daddy. "Did we have fun," he wrote. "This was the good ole days, when a man was a man and a chap (kid) was a chap and the ladies smoked cigars... The Madame is looking right pert, isn't she?" It's a postcard memento from an epic family visit to the MidSouth Fairgrounds Amusement Park in Memphis. Clockwise from top left are:
1. Cousin Virginia "Jinks" Cox, 2. Aunt Elizabeth "Ewee" Selman (with cigar?), 3. Daddy (with the biggest grin), 4. Momma (looking pert), 5. Sister Jett (who left us way too soon), 6. Brother "Wild Man" George (who saved me from looking the geekiest here), 7. California Cousin Brian "Butch" Jacobs (having "the best summer of my life"), 8. me (the geek in the straw hat), 9. California Cousin Jack "Bonehead" Selman, 10. Cousin Judy Cox and 11. Brother "Mannish Thang" Duke.

# PROLOGUE

## Back to Adam

In delving into the lore of my ancestors, I suddenly realized I've been descending from them for more years I'd ever dared to hope would be mine. Going forward, I've actually made it to the "back nine" of life and, unlike my golf score, I'm still descending.

Going backward, I've actually been able to trace my descent all the way back from Adam. This really can be done! No joke! You'll have to read Chapter 16 to see how.

I'm just glad I lived long enough to get it done. As a child, I didn't have a promising beginning, being plagued by asthma in the early years. I was allergic to the Mississippi Delta—and to farm work.

When I was fourteen, I read something about how the ancients in some cultures used to simply leave their weak and sickly infants outside in the wilderness for the lions to snack on. I'm glad this wasn't in the cards for *me*, because being *lionized* in that way doesn't sound too appetizing—except to the lions, of course.

Luckily, I've lived long enough to cross the last thing off my bucket list—writing this book. It has been a challenge, but it has been rewarding. At the last minute I received a photo I'd never seen before. The photo caption sums up the stroll I've been able to take down memory lane.

The shot shows Daddy at the MidSouth Fairgrounds in Memphis, surrounded by many of the people he loved best. He's in the middle, wearing the biggest grin. He wrote in the margin: "Did we have fun!"

We *did*, in spades!

Through these pages may Jack and Rob, my amazing sons, know better those who have paved the way.

My wish is that Jack and Rob, their wives, Amy and Adrienne, and my granddaughter—Jack and Amy's daughter, Shiloh—descend for a long, long time!

And *have fun* along the way!

# THE FIRST JACK?

J ♠

# THE ORIGIN OF
# OUR SPECIES?

# THE DEMISE OF OTHER SPECIES?

This Jack, my Daddy, was an enthusiastic hunter, to say the least.

Twenty And A Quarter Pounds Of Wild Gobble

The newspaper photo with the turkey, appeared in several publications,
including *The New York Times,* quoting Daddy as saying,
"The turkeys are plentiful and so are the mosquitoes."

# CHAPTER 1

## Jacks Full

---

### A stacked deck

My family-tree deck is stacked with Jacks, starting with my granddaddy, whose real name was George Day Perry.

His mother waited so long to name him and his older brother, Marshall Dabney Perry, that their father simply nicknamed them Pete and Jack, the names of the family's pair of stubborn mules.

Our branch of the family descended from Jack, as in jackass, which may have seemed accurate to my granddaddy's father, who often told the boy he wouldn't amount to much.

But failure was not in the cards for this boy Jack.

Although he started in a Tennessee log house, Granddaddy Jack eventually hit the jackpot. Along with his wife, Miss Sallie (the former Sallie Jett Whitley, descendant of a Norman knight), whose family had fallen on hard times, he amassed more than 17,000 acres of Mississippi Delta pay dirt, perhaps the richest farmland in the world.

They had six handsome, strapping sons, and three beautiful daughters. Their fourth son was Jack Whitley Perry, whom I called Daddy.

Daddy Jack was a real wild card until he got tamed by my mother, Georgia Pace. They settled down and Daddy was content to be a husband, father, planter, and hunter. But he always remained a joker.

Much of this story is about Daddy's humor. "He could have been another Bob Hope," said one of his sisters. She ought to have known, since she had moved from the family farm near Hollywood, Mississippi, to California homes in Hollywood and in Palm Desert, which is just a few miles from the Bob Hope home in Palm Springs.

At birth, I was named J Whitley Perry, which I curse every time I am

3

hounded by someone demanding to know what the J (with no period) stands for. They often guess at names like Jehosaphat or Jeremiah. Not only does J stand for nothing, but I go by Whit, which means "the smallest possible amount."

When I was baptized, the bishop of the Mississippi diocese of the Episcopal Church begged Daddy to "give the boy your name!" Daddy refused, saying he didn't want me called Junior or, even worse, Junius, in the parlance of the farm workers.

Besides, a cousin older than me had already been named Jack Day Perry. (He's called Jack Day and his son, Jack Day Perry Jr., is known as Brother Baby, courtesy of the farm hands.)

So I'm just J, a quarter of a Jack (or a quarter of a Delta Jack, since I only spent about a fourth of my life in The Delta).

My first son is named Jack Whitley Perry II, as a salute to Daddy Jack and to get the Jack tradition back on track.

The extended family is now loaded with other Jacks. One of the most colorful is Jack Perry Selman, known in the family as Bonehead. There are quite a few Georges, too, but even one of them goes by Jack.

I couldn't carry on the farming tradition of the first two Jacks, because I started out as an asthmatic runt. Daddy loved me, I'm sure, but he always told me, "You can't be a farmer."

When I was twenty-one, I headed east to find myself and I didn't stop until I had circled the globe, traveling alone across four continents for almost a year, hitchhiking whenever possible, and finally getting comfortable in my own skin. Like the Anthony Hopkins character who figures out a way to kill the relentless grizzly bear in the movie *The Edge,* I wanted to do something that was unequivocal.

You can go north or south and you will eventually reverse directions, but you can go east, chasing your tail, forever—even going back into time for a day when you cross the international date line. My trip east ultimately took me back to the South and The Delta's gravitational field, which often pulls at my memory.

I'm now going back in time to chase my *tale* and I'm *jacked up* about it. It's a tale worth saving from oblivion.

First, let me give you a glimpse into *who* Daddy Jack was.

He's the one with the cocked fedora hat, in the middle on the cover.

His daddy, the first Jack, is on the left, sporting a top hat. That's me, walking away, on the right.

## One matchless childhood moment

It was a scene that Daddy wanted indelibly stamped upon my young memory.

"Remember this," he urged, with a tinge of sadness as his blue eyes scanned the vault of dying light above the winter woods. "You'll never see anything like this again."

The sunset was electric with endless strings of ducks and geese swirling by the thousands in a vast symphony of whistling wings as formation after formation spiraled downward to beat the darkness to the wetlands below.

These flocks had funneled down from the Arctic reaches of Canada and Alaska, into the middle of the hourglass-shaped Mississippi River Flyway, where they congregated chaotically before fanning out into the warmer regions to the south.

I was in my first decade, awestruck by the majesty of it all. Daddy was at the end of his fifth decade, old enough to be my grandfather and anxious to teach me the ways of a world that was changing too fast for him.

Born in 1902, he had grown up in the Mississippi Delta when hunting meant putting protein on the dinner table.

As boys, he and his brothers had started with homemade hollow-cane pistols, armed with powder from dissected firecrackers. Daddy soon advanced to a cast-iron pipe and dissected shotgun shells. He'd insert a firecracker fuse into a small hole in the loaded pipe, light it, and hope his target would stick around for the explosion.

When Granddaddy called a halt to the arms race, Daddy crammed all his ammo into his pistol for one last glorious shot—which rocketed the pipe into his forehead and knocked him unconscious.

Granddaddy angrily gathered up all the guns and threw them into a fired-up potbelly stove. Luckily, he wasn't injured when the steel lids lifted off the stove in the ensuing explosion!

Daddy graduated to real guns just as all the big game was disappearing from The Delta. Tales of bears, panthers and wolves now live mostly in folklore.

## Into the wild

In March of 2008 I was fortunate to be able to sit down for a few hours with eighty-six-year-old Edgar M. "Son" Hood Jr., a retired Tunica County planter whose grandparents were pioneers in The Delta.

He told about their run-ins with predatory wildlife.

Bears often raided his grandparents' corn, leaving many corn-ear piles inside their split-rail fence. "They finally figured out that every time the bears would get to the fence with a load of corn they'd drop it as they tried to go over the fence. The bears would just leave the ears there and go get a fresh 'armload,'" he said.

"My grandmother was home alone one night when the chimney caught on fire. It was made of sticks and mud. She grabbed the baby in one arm and a bucket in the other hand and went out to get some water and found herself surrounded by wolves."

He said that she knew that if the house burned down she'd be even more vulnerable, so she just got the water, stared down the wolves, went back inside, and put the fire out.

One time his father, Edgar Hood Sr., was coming home with a wagonload of fresh meat. "He was about to go under a tree that was leaning over the road when his horse started neighing and bucking up and wouldn't go under the tree. He looked up in the tree and saw a panther, with his eyes glowing."

Mr. Hood said his father simply threw the meat off the wagon, giving it to the panther, and raced home, safe and sound.

All that was before Daddy's time, but the deer did disappear on his watch. Even the wild turkeys were on the way out, only to be saved by the conservation efforts of Daddy and his brothers.

Writer Wade S. Wineman Jr., in his *East of Slash* book on turkey hunting (OK Publishing Co., Greenville, MS), says, "Many locals believe that, because of the fear instilled in the poaching public by the Perrys, a good seed flock of turkeys was preserved while the rest of the state's flocks were being wiped out."

The family was famous (or infamous) for the posted signs they put up all over their woods. When Granddaddy died, one town wag said, "I hope Mr. Perry goes to hell! He'll have it posted in a week and nobody'll be able to get in!"

Before his death, Granddaddy acquired two bears and a trio of elk, as a reminder of what had been. When the bears attacked a farmhand who was assigned to feed them, the Memphis Zoo got two free bears.

The elk soon tired of their pasture and began leaping fences. My uncle Bobby Cox was assigned round-up duties but was slow saddling his horse one day. The elk were last reported twenty miles away, gone for good.

One day, years later, on a duck-hunting trip with Daddy, I spotted what I thought was a mule in the woods. We stopped the Jeep and finally made out a huge whitetail buck in the trees. The deer had returned—with a vengeance, we would learn later as their numbers swelled to "vermin" proportions.

The game warden begged us to kill one hundred one year. I came home from college and shot five in one day, including the equivalent of a golfing hole-in-one—a kill shot in the eye of a running deer more than one hundred yards away. Although I should have been happy about the miracle shot and the fact that I would feed five farm families for a month, I began to lose my zest for hunting. It just didn't feel fair.

Now I hunt with a camera.

Nearly every day wild geese pass a few feet over my house in LaGrange, Georgia. Sometimes, when I'm outside, I see their shadows or hear the rustling of wings before they pass overhead. I always feel blessed.

I've only made one goose kill, a childhood achievement that was completely ruined when the goose's partner circled back and bravely tried to assist its fatally wounded mate in getting off the water.

It was on another goose hunt that memorable day when Daddy prophesied, "You'll never see anything like this again!"

In sixty seven years I've seen lots of things, including many of the wonders of the world, ranging from the Egyptian pyramids to Mount Everest on the day the first American reached the summit. But nothing matches what I saw in the sky as a boy: a living aurora borealis made up of waterfowl!

I'm glad we killed no geese that day.

## The gravity of ghosts

Memories of Daddy tug at me when I least expect it.

There's a ghost calling in the chuckling of autumn leaves, and the pungent aroma of fresh-turned spring soil can seep into my subconscious and pull me back to another time and place.

The gravity of the past grabbed me once in a western North Carolina valley that the Cherokees called "the place of fresh green." It is surrounded by blue mountains stacked against the horizon in varying shades of smoke.

The place was the John C. Campbell Folk School, a school for adults founded in 1925 near Brasstown. The school's logo is a man walking behind a brace of horses, underscored by the text, "I sing behind the plow." These words are from a Danish folk song, which begins with: "I am just a common farmer…I sing behind the plow… for I am happy and free."

Standing by the forge in the blacksmith shop, smelling the burning coal and hearing the hammer thumping on the red-hot steel, I was transported to the farm forge of my youth where I'd spent many a lazy day making tomahawks and frog gigs under the tutelage of the farm blacksmith.

I remembered riding around our Mississippi Delta farm with Daddy, who was always singing—for he was happy and free. For a moment I understood, fully.

Daddy's singing slipped up on me another time.

On a helicopter flight over the Smoky Mountains I spotted an enclave of old homesteads in a secluded cove. When I landed, I got in my car and drove to the site.

Called Cade's Cove, it was once an isolated community of hardy farming families. It now stands silent—its churches and homes empty, its fields tended with modern machinery to preserve a living snapshot of a long-gone frontier culture.

The cove's families were kicked off their land so their island in the forest could become an outdoor museum within the Great Smoky Mountains National Park, preserved for tourists—like me.

The visit was marred by mobs of sightseers, caravanning through in a slow, serpentine procession, stopping each time a pine cone fell and seeming to ask themselves, "What was *that*, a *deer* or a *bear?*"

Suddenly I spotted a side road that cut across the fields in the middle of the large tourist loop. Slipping out of the snaking skein of sightseers, I soon found my pulse slowing. I slowed to a crawl, surrounded on both sides by fields of gold.

A deer bobbed its head up from the waves of grain, then melted back down into the depths. It was warm. Late-summer insects were making their music. I stopped.

From way down in my memory, a song formed on my lips: "Smile the while I kiss you sad adieu; when the clouds roll by I'll come to you..."

It was *Till We Meet Again*, a song that composer Richard Whiting and lyricist Raymond Egan felt had so little commercial potential they threw the manuscript into a wastebasket. According to one story, Mrs. Whiting fished it out and took it to a publisher. It became the most popular ballad of World War I.

Daddy never was a soldier, but he knew a good tune and he had a great tenor voice. He sang this song often when I would ride around the farm with him. "...Every tear will be a memory. So wait and pray each night for me, till we meet again."

For a moment the clock rolled back more than half a century. I smiled. I was a kid again on a Delta cotton farm. A peace beyond understanding passed over me.

The clouds rolled by. I pressed the pedal and eased back into the circling line of sizzling summer traffic, out of the cove and out of the park, re-entering the fray of life with a renewed spirit.

# Delta Pioneers Braved This...

*A flood refugee camp on the levee*

*A levee break*

# ...To Get This

*Rich cotton harvests...*

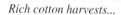

*...and virgin timber*

# CHAPTER 2

## Against the Odds

### Ground zero

Now, let me introduce you to another central character, the Mississippi-Yazoo Delta. For simplicity I will simply refer to it as The Delta.

In his book, *Where I Was Born and Raised* (Boston: Houghton Mifflin Company, 1948), Delta native David L. Cohn famously quipped that The Delta really starts, in spirit, in Tennessee, in the lobby of a historic Memphis hotel known as the Peabody, and ends about two hundred miles to the south on Vicksburg, Mississippi's Catfish Row, "a typical gathering-place for Negroes," with its dice games, "aroma of love," and "soul-satisfying scent of catfish frying" (pp. 12-14).

I would not exist without the Peabody. Famous for its rooftop dances and the mallard ducks that swim in the lobby fountain, the Peabody once was a magnet for Mississippi Delta cotton planters, who came north to socialize and to cut deals.

The Peabody lobby was the place where Daddy, a bachelor planter, met Momma, who was working as a Peabody hatcheck girl. She found it to be much more exciting than her previous job as a Woolworth's five-and-dime clerk.

The lobby was the crossroads of two lines of ancestry: hers, which went back to a refugee from Ireland's potato famine; and his, which stretched back to a Norman knight and European royalty.

To Momma, Daddy was a knight in shining armor. To Daddy, Momma was "the prettiest girl in the world," a slogan he penned on her swimsuit photo, which was taken when she won the title of Miss Peabody in a beauty competition.

After a whirlwind romance, they were married. They are now buried side by side in the dark rich soil that was the foundation of their fifty-two-year marriage.

Before I tell their story, I need to tell you about The Delta, which has evolved into much more than the swampy woodland of yore—a very unlikely place to succeed. First, let's take a look at the birth of another very risky business proposition, America.

## A history of land lust

Much of my ancestors' lust for land was rooted in the oppressive European system of limited land ownership, where the elite were lords of the earth. Those fortunate to own land usually left it to the first-born son, so the family wouldn't have to break it into smaller parcels.

This led to waves of titled and non-titled English, Welsh, Scots, and Irish immigrants filtering into the nooks and crannies of the American landscape, staking claims and sometimes fouling the nest and moving west. It is their independent spirit that made this country what it is today.

This spirit fueled my Perry grandparents' unlikely success story. To fully understand the story you have to go back in time to when the transition of land ownership, from red men to white men, really began in earnest—with the Jamestown colonists, who were basically a ragtag bunch of illegal aliens in pursuit of economic gain in a New World lottery.

Forget Disney's mythological take on the story. According to one scholar, Pocahontas was a nickname meaning "little cruel undisciplined brat."

Captain John Smith, by many accounts, was an obnoxious braggart and bully, who twice narrowly escaped being hanged by his own people.

Yet, somehow this unlikely cast of characters forged its way into our hearts and history, arriving twelve years before the Plymouth Pilgrims and forty-two years after Spaniards founded St. Augustine, Florida.

In celebrating Jamestown's founding, more than four hundred years ago, we are saluting a business proposition that evolved into our business-driven nation—which, like Jamestown, is a miracle based on bravado and wit.

In 1607 the colonists, 104 men and boys, sailed into Chesapeake

Bay aboard three ships, finding fair meadows, tall trees, and fresh, running water.

They happened to settle on a river island a few miles from the headquarters of a centuries-old culture ruled by Powhatan, a Native American chieftain who headed a cobbled-together federation of tribes with a population of about fifteen thousand.

And that wasn't the colonists' only problem. They arrived during a seven-year drought, say scientists who have studied the area's tree-ring history.

The colonists had scarcely been there two weeks when the Indians attacked, only to be repelled by cannon fire. Two settlers died and the survivors got extremely motivated to build a fort, completing a triangular stockade around an acre of land in just nineteen days.

Exhausted and deprived of fresh water, the men soon succumbed to disease and starvation.

### A work ethic rooted in adversity

Pushing his "If you don't work, you don't eat!" philosophy, Smith, who was twenty-seven, showed the resolve that eventually made him president of the colony. This Machiavellian, self-taught soldier hated bluebloods—a contempt that earned him a death sentence.

When he was spared and assigned to lead a search party to find and meet with the Indians, some colonists hoped he would not return.

Captured and brought before Chief Powhatan, Smith awed his captors with the magic of compass and gunpowder, noting that the Indians seized his gunpowder with the idea of planting and growing it.

According to Smith, the Indians were set to club him to death when one of the chief's daughters, Pocahontas, intervened. There is no record of this except Smith's own account. According to historians, this could have been just a ritual in which a woman is foreordained to "save" someone just before he is adopted into the tribe.

Nevertheless, Smith was adopted and returned triumphantly to Fort James with a life-saving larder.

For seven months things went splendidly—until fall, when the Indians cut off the food supply to prepare for winter. Smith returned their kindness with food raids, burning and looting as he went, even kidnapping Pocahontas, who remained at the fort for a year, converted to Christianity, and later married John Rolfe after being told that Smith, who had left, was dead.

She became ill and died, disappointed, soon after being taken to England, where she discovered that Smith was very much alive.

This early history isn't pretty, but the Jamestown colonists eventually prospered—even though, as Smith noted in his journals, they were "ten times more fit to spoil a commonwealth than…to begin one."

## The British keep a-coming

Although the colonists' death rate was about 75 percent the first seventeen years, the Anglos kept coming, fleeing poverty and overpopulation at home.

By 1650, the Native American population, beset by whites and new diseases, had plummeted from 1,002,000 in "pre-contact" eastern North America to less than 400,000, according to a map insert in the May 2007 issue of *National Geographic*.

In 1650 there were 58,000 Europeans throughout the east, the magazine says, noting that indentured servants were gradually being replaced by African slaves, which numbered only 1600 in 1650.

*National Geographic* estimates that by 1800 there were only 178,000 Indians remaining in the east, while the Europeans had skyrocketed to 4,763,000 and the Africans had grown to 1,002,000—matching the Indians' pre-contact total.

According to the article "Inventing America" by Richard Brookhiser in the April 26, 2007, issue of *TIME* magazine, Jamestown "contained in embryo the same contradictions that still resonate in America today—the tension between freedom and authority, between public purpose and private initiative, between our hopes and our fears."

The story goes on today, warts and all.

## The Trail of Tears

Part-Cherokee Jim Dykes, writing in 1985 about the Trail of Tears of the 1830s in the December 15, 1985, issue of the *Atlanta Weekly* magazine of the *Atlanta Journal-Constitution* ("The Trail of Tears," pp. 13-41), says that when King James in the early 1600s stocked Ireland with "sturdy Scots," it set the stage for the American removal of the southeastern Indian tribes.

Dykes wrote that the Irish Catholics and the Scottish Protestants fought each other constantly and eventually took their fighting spirit to the Americas, starting about 1720, earnestly believing that they deserved the frontier lands more than the Indians.

It is not a pretty chapter in our history. Said Red Cloud of the Sioux: "They (the whites) made us many promises. More than I can remember. But they never kept but one. They promised they would take our land and they took it."

Dykes said that President Andrew Jackson was "just the engineer" of Indian removal. He says the "architect" was Thomas Jefferson, who wrote to William Henry Harrison in 1803, "We shall push our trading houses and be glad to see the good and influential individuals among them run in debt, because we observed that when these debts get beyond what the individual can pay, they become willing to lop them off by cession of lands."

This was certainly not Jefferson's noblest writing. In a bit of possibly unintentional symbolism, the U.S. Mint eventually allowed Jefferson to push the Indian off the face of the Buffalo Nickel. Perhaps the coin should have Jefferson's face on both sides.

## Westward ho

Soon after America became official in 1776, many of my ancestors began to leave their farms in Virginia and the Carolinas, pushing into the new frontiers to the west. Many had degraded the soils of their plantations and were looking for new lands where they could utilize their burgeoning slave populations.

Some were poor pioneers pushing west with only their families in tow, hoping some day to have farms of their own.

The fertile soils of West Tennessee proved a magnet for many, including dropouts from groups just passing through. The southwestern part of Tennessee is where many of my paternal forebears carved out their fiefdoms, beginning in the early 1830s, just across the Mississippi River from the territory acquired by America though the 1803 Louisiana Purchase.

At this time a few brave farmers had just begun filtering into the vast Delta swampland jungle to the south. (Even the Chickasaw and Choctaw Indians had begun farming European-style, and some owned slaves before they ceded their territories to the whites—or, later, were evicted.)

## A wholesale villain

The whites moved down the Mississippi River and started settlements along the banks.

One of these was a remote location along a loop in the river along the Tunica-DeSoto County, Mississippi, line, which became known as Council Bend—because it was the meeting place of a Tennessee-born desperado named John Murrell and his band of some one thousand desperate outlaws, called the Mystic Brotherhood. Mark Twain compared Murrell to Jesse James, noting that James was "retail" and Murrell was "wholesale."

Murrell's father was a preacher, but his mother prostituted herself when her husband was away and taught her son to steal from her clientele at an early age.

Young John was handsome and smart and became a consummate con man, soon heading up a gang that ranged from Tennessee to New Orleans, stealing anything of value, including slaves, whom he stole and resold multiple times, cutting them in on the take until they got too well known—at which time they were murdered.

He often had his gang steal a congregation's horses while he "preached" and became known as "Reverend Devil." He was finally captured in 1844, and was pardoned after serving only fourteen years in a Tennessee prison, even though his exploits included murder.

He reportedly worked as a blacksmith in Pikeville, Tennessee, until his death a few years later. Some say he faked his own death and disappeared.

It has been said that his capture undermined a slave revolt he had been planning in an effort to take over the South. As Mark Twain said, he was "wholesale."

## Nibbling at the edges

As settlers began forming new river towns, they began nibbling at the edges of the Delta's vine-infested tangle of canebrakes and climax forests—a vast expanse of old-growth trees, many of which were six feet or more in diameter. There were cypress, sweet gum, tupelo, pecan, walnut, persimmon, ash, hickory, hackberry, cottonwood, and poplar, to name a few.

Teams of "deadeners" attacked with axes, stripping rings of bark off the trees to kill them for easier removal or burning. The push to clear and drain the land had started, launching a quest that would be assisted by the later arrival of levees and railroads. It was a push to fulfill a prediction from the state geologist of Mississippi that The Delta would become "the garden spot of North America—where wealth and prosperity culminate."

It was a very slow process. By the 1860's, only about ten percent of The Delta had been cleared, and much of that reverted to weeds after the Civil War. After undergoing the chaos of the post-war Reconstruction period, planters again began to attack the swampland forests in the late 1800s, setting the stage for my grandparents to move to Mississippi and join the challenge of wresting very profitable farmland from the wilderness at the turn of the century. As William Faulkner said, it was to be "deswamped, denuded and derivered in two generations."

It would not be a walk in the park.

## The dirt on the dirt

Since the real business of The Delta is the business of dirt, let me now give you the real dirt on this storied place, described by writer Richard Ford as "The South's South," and called "The Most Southern Place on Earth," the title of a book by James C. Cobb. It has also been called "the cream jug of the continent" and "the bowl of the gods." Writer David L. Cohn called it "a strange and detached fragment thrown off by the whirling comet that is America."

When you leave the rolling hills of southwestern Tennessee, heading south on legendary Highway 61 from Memphis, a city literally built on a bluff, you suddenly find yourself dropping down onto a flat, seemingly endless plain of farm fields that runs for about two hundred miles to the south. It's quite a dramatic entrance, if you can ignore all the casino billboards.

The soil is black and rich, presenting panoramas that change with the seasons from the greenery of spring to a white blanket of cotton in the fall.

Off to your west (your right) there begins a levee, part of a system of huge dirt walls that zigzag southward on both sides of the river for hundreds of miles. They defend against the vast, serpentine string of swirling maelstroms known as the "Father of Waters," the mighty Mississippi River (an alternate, perhaps more accurate, Indian name is the "Son of Many Fathers").

Were it not for the levees, your trip would be a wet proposition, particularly during spring floods.

Currently averaging 40 feet high and 350 feet wide at the base, with gentle grass-covered slopes, the levees have been put up and washed away countless times. The current battle is being waged by the US Army Corps of Engineers, which also must continually dredge silt out of the river to keep shipping channels open.

It is said that the levee system can be seen by astronauts from space, second in man-made prominence only to the Great Wall of China.

## Those damned dams

The levees, which recently burst into infamy far to the south when Hurricane Katrina devastated New Orleans, date back to Jean Baptiste Le Moyne, Sieur de Bienville (which may be French for "idiotic aristocrat").

As governor of French Louisiana, he went against his engineers' advice (and Biblical teachings about questionable foundations) and handpicked the site for the city of New Orleans in a mosquito-infested, below-sea-level bend of the Mississippi River between the Gulf of Mexico and Lake Pontchartrain.

Unbeknownst to him, he picked the small end of one of the largest land-based water funnels in the world, the focal point of an unbelievably vast drain basin.

Founded in 1718, New Orleans was harried by four hurricanes in its first four years. In 1723 work was started on their first futile levee.

Now there is a system of earthen dikes all up and down the river. Engineers struggle to keep a navigable channel, continually shoring up the banks with riprap debris and dredging the main channels every time the waters try to change course. The landscape along the river is streaked with long crescent-shaped lakes and U-shaped oxbow lakes where the river used to run.

Stand on the river's banks and you witness one roiling mess, flecked with foam, full of swirling eddies and whirlpools. Sometimes you can even see eddies moving upstream, seemingly against the laws of physics.

When the river floods, it puts tremendous pressure on the levees and can even seep through the base, forming boils (bubbling leaks) on the other side.

In 1897 the levee broke in Tunica County at Flour Bend, so named because a barge full of flour once sank there, briefly turning the river white. The bend is now called *Flower* Lake, formed when the river changed course.

Tunica planter and merchant F. M. Norfleet witnessed the levee break, explaining that a small break in the levee started a few inches wide and rapidly progressed to the size of a stovepipe, a water bucket, and then a barrel.

"Before I could even mentally describe it, the whole top of the levee was twisting in," Norfleet later reported. "Then the water was forcing its way through in a great torrent, and striking the ground beyond the base of the levee with terrific force, rebounding in awful anger, white waves 20 feet high, tearing great oak and gum trees out by the roots and tossing them about as if they were cork.

"The ends of the levee began to erode quickly on either side of the break until well over fifteen acres were torn out like a great well, with holes and pits, some of them fifty feet deep.

"I have been in front of the cannon's mouth, and have heard the rattle of musketry and the whistling of bullets, but I had never felt such an awful dread," he added.

The water gouged out the very deep Blue Hole, which later became a popular swimming spot on the river side of the levee.

The sand, which was scoured out when the hole was formed, spread out over two hundred acres of farmland, rendering it useless for years until massive doses of animal fertilizer and other organic matter made it fertile again, said Tunica planter Edgar M. Hood Jr.

Norfleet commented that "The rushing, swirling, tumbling waters were at the same time a sight of wondrous grandeur and appalling solemnity." This brings to mind a remark from William Faulkner, posted on a wall of the Tunica Museum: "The river was doing what it liked to do, just as a mule will work for you for ten years for the privilege of kicking you once."

## Head for the hills

Mr. Hood said that, years later, the high water in 1937 prompted planters to send their mules to the hills and their wives and children to Memphis until the crisis passed.

"My Daddy said, 'Son, if that levee breaks I'm broke.' He had a million feet of what they called five-quarter hardwood lumber on sticks, drying. We were cutting that lumber in a steam-driven sawmill for Fisher Body in Memphis, because that's what they were using for making automobiles."

He said that when a log was too big to fit the sawmill equipment, they would drill holes in it and set off black-powder explosions inside the log to split it into smaller, more manageable sections. "We were counting on this lumber to save us from the Depression," Hood said. "When the water reached record flood stage we had to have armed guards patrol the levee and we had to put down sandbags when boils appeared."

The solution to boils is to put a dam of sandbags around the holes until the seeping water gets as high as the floodwaters on the other side. This equalizes the pressure and stops the holes from growing.

The Tunica levees held that year, as well as ten years earlier, in 1927, when massive flooding occurred to the south when the levee ruptured at Scott, Mississippi, and the swollen river inundated the southern half of The Delta, pushing eastward for sixty miles and southward for ninety.

In his autobiography, *Lanterns on the Levee* (Baton Rouge: Louisiana State University Press, 1977), William Alexander Percy had this to say: "The 1927 flood was a torrent ten feet deep the size of Rhode Island; it was thirty-six hours coming and four months going; it was deep enough to drown a man, swift enough to upset a boat, and lasting enough to cancel a crop year" (p. 249).

Why would anyone want to live in this flood plain? Having spent the first fourteen years of my life in a farmhouse in the shadow of the levee in the northwestern corner of The Delta, all I can say is, "Because of its rich, dark soil and its even richer, colorful culture."

My family thrived on perhaps the world's greatest farming land. Daddy thought it was the best place on earth, in spite of myriad maladies relating to manpower, mules, mud, mosquitoes, and malaria, not to mention weather, worms, and weevils.

As historian Shelby Foote, a Greenville native, once quipped, you could experience "a hundred years of history in twenty years in The Delta."

## No joking matter

We used to joke that sometimes the river got so high you could see *under* it. But when we'd look at the other side of the levee during a particularly high spring flood, it was no joking matter.

Often the water would gouge holes into the levee deep enough for my brothers and me to play hide-and-seek until swarms of trucks, cranes, and bulldozers came to repair the damage.

We spent a lot of time fishing and hunting in the woods and lakes between the river and the levee, sometimes grappling for fish in the muddy backwaters with our bare hands.

On my sixth birthday Daddy took me fishing on one of these lakes, paddling me around, baiting my hook, and stringing my fish. In about an hour I had caught more than fifty fish, including primitive alligator gars, catfish, buffalo, drum, carp, bream, crappie, bass, and grennels or bowfins, which we called "grinners." I even caught a one-inch-long bream when it somehow, miraculously, did a headstand on a bare hook which had dropped into the water while Daddy was stringing another fish.

Just how tenuous the levees are is spelled out in *Rising Tide* by John M. Barry (New York: Simon & Schuster, 1998), whose amazing history of the river leading up to the great flood of 1927 explains that efforts to contain the river between levees have simply given the river permission to raise its floor and continue to be a threat.

### Homegrown terrorism

And then there are the threats from people. Daddy used to tell about the time when a levee burst across the river in Arkansas and he was conscripted and armed to patrol a section of "our" levee to keep the Arkansans from dynamiting it in a gracious effort to share the water wealth.

Ironically, this is exactly what the city fathers of New Orleans did to their neighbors in 1927. Barry says that the "powers that be" in New Orleans made a decision that they would dynamite the levee outside the city, mainly to protect various financial interests.

They promised to pay for any damages to those who were flooded, but reneged mostly, leaving some fourteen thousand people homeless.

So maybe Mother Nature has served up some kind of poetic justice with Katrina.

It would make sense to abandon the whole soggy mess, name it

Lake New Orleans, and move on, but our hearts and the weight of history feed arguments against that notion.

The Spanish seized the site from the French. Napoleon took it back, then sold it to the fledgling United States as part of the fifteen-million-dollar Louisiana Purchase. Our last battle against the British occurred there when a human gumbo of whites, Creoles, Indians, blacks, and even pirates banded together to make a definitive American statement.

Jazz was born there. Mardi Gras put a let-the-good-times-roll face on the Big Easy. It's our country's largest port, where some seventy million tons of goods pass each year.

Equally damaging was the breach in the dam of civilization, revealing how thin the veneer really is. Katrina ruptured the scant skin of sanity that we like to think protects us all, giving credence to the saying that "Life is what happens when you're making other plans."

## LOSERS

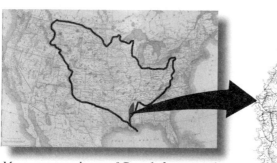

Many states and part of Canada **lost** topsoil.

## WINNERS

MEMPHIS

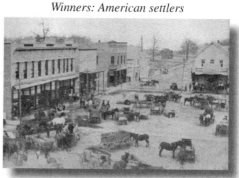

VICKSBURG

The Mississippi-Yazoo Delta **gained** topsoil

*Losers: Native Americans, Spaniards*

*This romanticized painting, attempting to show De Soto's discovery of the Mississippi River, is entirely incorrect, from the plains-type teepees to the native garb.*

*Winners: American settlers*

*Winners: Engineers*

*Losers: Wildlife*

*Winner: "Teddy Bear," the doll which was created after Teddy Roosevelt, on a Delta hunt, refused to shoot a young bear.*

# CHAPTER 3

## Winners and Losers

### A state of mind

Entering Mississippi south of Memphis on Highway 61, you first come to DeSoto County, named in honor of Spanish explorer Hernando de Soto, who lost his life soon after "discovering" the river in which his mortal remains were submerged (in an effort to keep the Indians from finding out that the Spaniard was a mere mortal).

To your left is a line of hills that runs south-southeasterly away from you, forming the eastern border of a flat geographical and psychological phenomenon known as The Delta. Technically it's the floodplain of the Mississippi and Yazoo Rivers.

There are deltas all over the world, formed where rivers fan out and deposit dirt into larger bodies of water, building up sediment, but this is *THE* Delta, the fabled land of blues music and blurry myth, which flow through the land like some unstoppable stream of consciousness. Much more than a plot of earth, The Delta is also a state of mind.

### Pay dirt

Continuing south on Highway 61 you next come to the place where I grew up, Tunica County, now awash in a new kind of pay dirt—enough casinos to rival Atlantic City!

Tunica, which had a population that was 85 percent African American in 1930, has come a long way from later being crowned "the poorest county in the United States," and its county government seems hard put to spend all its tax revenue, luxuriating in improvements that range from a commercial airport to a couple of new museums, including one on the riverbank.

The riverbank museum features a dramatic display illustrating how deep the county's topsoil is. There are long, transparent plastic tubes hanging from the ceiling, filled with various combinations of topsoil, sand, and rocks. Each tube represents some famous farming section of the United States.

The topsoil tubes include New Mexico at four inches, Vermont at three feet, Texas at four feet, and Illinois at six feet. The winner, by a landslide, is the tube representing the Mississippi Delta topsoil—twenty-eight feet deep! I've heard some farmers speculate that in places this measurement would only scratch the surface.

More astounding is where all that topsoil came from. When I was a boy I found the answer in my grandfather's huge library, which he began stocking with tomes from estate sales.

The answer was spelled out in a 640-page book, *Riparian Lands of the Mississippi River* (New Orleans: Frank H. Tompkins, 1901). The title sounds romantic, but "riparian" simply means "of or relating to a riverbank."

In the middle of the book is a foldout US map "showing the area drained into the Mississippi River," indicated by a red line. The river, according to the book, "drains a territory whose area equals in extent the combined area of Austria, Germany, Holland, France, Italy, Portugal, Spain, Norway and Great Britain… This vast drainage area, 1,256,000 square miles in extent, is equal to nearly one-half of the total area of the United States. It touches 30 States, 2 (Indian) Territories and 2 Provinces of British possessions (Canada).

"…At flood time the discharge (of water) amounts to two million cubic feet per second," and carries vast quantities of sediment gathered from an area stretching from the Rocky Mountains in the remote Northwest to the Alleghenies in the East.

Since 100 percent of Tunica County's 271,731 acres is made up of alluvial (deposited) land, you could say I grew up *on* thirty states, from Montana to New York—and even a bit of Canada.

The county's population, the book says, was 8,461 in 1880, and the assessed value of all the county's land was $89,251. By 1890 the population had doubled and the land value had jumped to approximately $1.5 million.

Granddaddy Jack grabbed his share, starting from scratch and eventually ending up with anywhere from seventeen thousand to twenty thousand acres, depending on which account you listen to. He and his wife-and-partner "Miss Sallie" also did their share of adding to the population, raising nine children. Miraculously, all nine survived into old age, with three making it into their nineties.

Their current living descendants exceed one hundred. (Counting remarriages, I had nineteen aunts and uncles on my father's side and another nineteen on my mother's side, thirty-eight altogether.)

One of my Perry cousins recently was trying to put together a billion-dollar-plus casino deal, which was to include an indoor eighteen-hole golf course.

## The whirlwinds of Commerce

Before the whirlwind of casino commerce hit the county, there was another whirlwind, which struck the same area where many of the casinos are built, near the site of a long-gone town known as Commerce.

When I was a boy there was a gravel road that ran straight away from another town, Robinsonville, and dead-ended at the levee, where you could take a dirt road over the levee to the former site of Commerce. This riverboat-landing town once had been bigger than Memphis, boasting a population of about seven thousand before the river gobbled up much of the town property, prompting abandonment of the rest.

One summer day, when I was ten, I went to visit Jimmy Carsley, whose father was a state trooper, living in Robinsonville. Jimmy and I decided to walk all the way to the levee, miles and miles past the rows of tenant houses on each side, past the Leatherman plantation home built on a mound that had been built as a raised home-site adjacent to an old Indian mound.

Some have speculated that the Leatherman Indian mound was where de Soto discovered the Mississippi River, but Tunica Museum executive director Dick Taylor feels that the more likely site is just to the south.

He dismisses Memphis' claim to the event, joking that some

Memphians would have you believe de Soto visited the ducks in the lobby of the Peabody. He cites one Spaniard's description of looking down from hills onto a vast, flat sea of treetops before traveling downward to an Indian town near the river. (You don't walk down from a hill to get to Memphis; it's on a bluff.)

Jimmy Carsley and I didn't care where de Soto did what. We were on our own exploratory mission. We went over the levee and into the woods.

We were looking for ruins, but the river had left few signs of civilization. The only interesting thing we could find was a hog-nosed snake, known as a puff adder for the way it puffs up just before it rolls over and plays dead with its mouth wide open. After we got through playing with the live "dead" snake, we made the long, hot walk home.

The peace along that road would be shattered less than a year later.

## An ominous cloud

On February 1, 1955, when I was thirteen, I was boarding the school bus in Tunica when I noticed an ominous black cloud in the direction of Robinsonville. The cloud was unlike any I'd seen before.

When I got home, Daddy was driving off in a hurry. He stopped and urged me to get in. A few miles later we found ourselves in the wake of an F3 tornado that had tracked eight miles from near Robinsonville to the river, at Commerce Landing, killing twenty people and injuring 141.

Before we got to the main area of devastation we stopped to talk to an old black man, who told us the wind had sucked his feet into the air as he desperately clung to a small tree. He was unhurt.

Then we got to the road that I had walked down the year before. The slope of the levee was dotted with debris and dead cows. The trees on the other side of the levee were mowed off at levee height, with sheets of roofing tin wrapped around most of the remaining stubs. A school for black children was demolished.

We then drove along the road toward Robinsonville. We stopped at the Abbay & Leatherman plantation office, where we were told the one constant line from tornado survivors: "It sounded like a freight train." (Which begs the question: What did tornadoes sound like before the train was invented?)

We marveled at the sights on both sides of the road. Some houses were completely gone, some were half gone (with furniture still in place in some rooms), and others were unharmed.

The wreckage was everywhere, and Daddy quickly decided I didn't need to see any more, taking me home. I guess he went back, alone, to see if he could help.

## The casino whirlwind

I'm glad that Daddy died before the area was hit by the whirlwind of casino commerce.

By the time this happened, Jimmy Carsley was a retired law-enforcement officer. The last time I saw him he was lured out of retirement to head up security for Splash, the first of many casinos, located a few miles south of Commerce Landing at Mhoon Landing, close to the family farm.

The casino was started in 1992 by businessmen who noted that Mississippi law allowed riverboat gambling. They decided to ram a barge up a slough (pronounced "slew") during the river's flood stage. They then dammed the slough, built a gaming house on the huge, flat-topped metal barge, and added support buildings on dry land, and the Tunica County gambling boom was ignited.

Although the gambling barge wasn't technically on the river, it was floating on water *from* the river, so it was deemed legal.

Splash was so popular that customers waited in line for hours to pay $10 apiece just to get in the door—in order to give the casino some more money.

Treating me to a steak dinner at Splash, Jimmy said that he understood that the casino had grossed more than $100 million in its first year.

## A big pie

Soon others wanted a piece of the pie. More sloughs were dredged, barges were floated in, and other casinos followed, including a true riverboat and a barge-based Bally's operation.

There was a building boom, which almost drove my farming brothers out of The Delta. Work crews were taking shortcuts through the farm. Cattle went missing. Drunks, one of them a nude woman, turned up in one brother's yard, sleeping it off.

My brothers bought another farm about twenty-five miles away, just in case, but suddenly the eye of this storm moved away to the north end of the county. A cluster of new casinos went up on various sloughs near Commerce. Gradually more were added north of there, with Grand Casino being the northernmost. Grand had an advantage, since it was closest to Memphis, until Tunica County built its own commercial airport, capable of handling big passenger jets.

## Gone with the wind

The name Robinsonville is fading now, in favor of Tunica Resorts, a wider area that includes nine casinos.

I recently went prowling around the old Mhoon Landing site, only to find weed-filled parking lots, the skeleton of the old Bally's support building filled with vandalized gambling machines, and a huge steel ship, empty and rusting away in a man-made trench.

Some local folks hope that the owners will restore the site to its previous wetlands condition, but there's little evidence to indicate they're in any rush to do so.

The old gravel road from Robinsonville to Commerce is now a four-lane parkway. The area boasts the tallest building in Mississippi, a casino hotel built on the river side of the levee, basically on dried swampland.

Many Tunica residents think the progress is wonderful, while others wouldn't mind a bit if the whole thing got blown into the river and flushed downstream to the Gulf of Mexico.

## "The Crossroads" legend

It's ironic that many people think Tunica County may have cut a deal with the devil, since Commerce Road (now Casino Strip Boulevard) may have been the site of another legendary deal—although at least three other sites lay claim to being "The Crossroads" of music legend.

The story involves blues icon Robert Johnson, considered by some to be the Grandfather of Rock and Roll. He lived as a teenager on the Abbay & Leatherman plantation in the Robinsonville area and prowled the nearby juke joints, listening to the likes of bluesmen Son House and Willie Brown.

The Tunica Museum says the story starts when Son House berated Johnson after his first public appearance in Robinsonville, saying, "Don't do that, Robert. You drive the people nuts. You can't play nothing!"

Johnson disappeared and, when he returned about six months later, House and Brown were astonished at Johnson's newly acquired skills, which surpassed theirs. In keeping with an old African myth, it was rumored that Johnson had sold his soul to the devil at a crossroads at midnight in exchange for musical dexterity. It was said the spirit even may have tuned his guitar.

Johnson called himself a "Steady Rollin' Man" and became an itinerant musician during the Depression era, even expanding into pop tunes such as *Tumbling Tumbleweeds* and *My Blue Heaven*. The entirety of his blues output (a total of twenty-nine original songs, including his classic *Sweet Home Chicago*) was recorded during five days of sessions in 1936 and 1937. The next year he died, at twenty-eight, after being poisoned at a Delta juke for getting too intimate with someone else's woman.

Johnson was inducted in 1986 into the Rock and Roll Hall of Fame, which states on its museum web site:

"Robert Johnson stands at the crossroads of American music... linking the country blues of the Mississippi Delta with the city blues of the post-World War II era. Johnson was a songwriter of searing depth and a guitar player with a commanding ability that inspired no less an admirer than Keith Richards of the Rolling Stones to exclaim,

'When I first heard [him], I was hearing two guitars, and it took me a long time to realize he was actually doing it all by himself.'"

Wikipedia says Johnson's "vocal phrasing, original songs, and guitar style have influenced a broad range of musicians, including Muddy Waters, Bob Dylan, Jimi Hendrix, Led Zeppelin, The Rolling Stones, Jeff Beck, Jack White, and Eric Clapton…"

Clapton called Johnson "the most important blues musician who ever lived."

## The roots of rock and roll

Some of Johnson's music was sexually raw, such as these "automotive" lyrics from *Terraplane Blues*:

> I'm gonna heist your hood, mama,
> I'm bound to check your oil…
> I'm going to get deep down in the connection,
> Keep on tangling with your wires,
> And when I mash down on your little starter,
> Then your spark plug will give me fire.

But the blues were about more than sex.

They had evolved from spirituals and "field holler" work chants, erupting from the Delta soil "like some, exotic, night-blooming vine bearing flowers of evil, sin, redemption, earthy sexuality and wild humor, all to the tune of guitars that moaned with notes drawn from African scales," wrote David Fulmer in his October 5, 2008 *Atlanta Journal-Constitution* review of Ted Gioia's new book, *Delta Blues: The Life and Times of the Mississippi Masters who Revolutionized American Music.*

In *Preachin' Blues* Robert Johnson says,

> The blues is a lowdown shakin' chill,
> You ain't never had them, I hope you never will.
> Well, the blues is a aching old heart disease
> Like consumption, chillin' me by degree[s].

The blues flowed into the North, carried there by black migrants who found new forms of alienation and disillusionment—and new urban audiences, who understood what the bluesmen were getting at. It has its roots in farming, but it wasn't about farming. It was about alienation.

Noted music preservationist and "song hunter" Alan Lomax, in his memoir, *The Land Where the Blues Began* (New York: Pantheon, 1993), said, "Years before the rest of the world, the people of The Delta tasted the bittersweet of modern alienation so that the blues of those days ring true for all of us now" (p. 11).

In the 1950s the bluesman's wail of alienation would seep into the collective soul of America. It was in Memphis in 1951 when Sam Phillips, owner of Sun Records, began to capture lightning on vinyl, starting with *Rocket 88* by the Delta band Knights of Rhythm. Some claim it was the first "rock and roll" record.

Also in 1951, the New York-based Dominoes came out with their overtly sexual *Sixty Minute Man*, "the first rhythm and blues song to 'cross over' to the pop charts," according to James C Cobb in his book, *The Most Southern Place on Earth* (New York: Oxford University Press, 1994). In the lyrics, the singer claims to "rock 'em and roll 'em all night long" (p.300).

Cobb writes that it wasn't long before Sam Phillips set out to find a white singer with "the Negro feel" and discovered Elvis Presley, whose first record had *Blue Moon of Kentucky*, a jazzed-up bluegrass song, on one side and *That's All Right Mama,* a blues tune, on the other side (pp. 300-301).

The "devil's music" was unleashed on the world, and the rest is history. Gradually, as rock and roll became respectable, it moved from its blues roots, only to be brought back on course by the British Invasion—the Rolling Stones, the Yardbirds, the Animals, Eric Clapton, etc.

It's ironic that the music born of gnawing despair and poverty would find such a following among relatively well-off white youth. It spoke to them, too—to a different sort of alienation. (In another bit of irony, many blacks abandoned the increasingly popular blues in favor of rap.)

And it all started in The Delta, right in my backyard, so to speak, with the likes of Robert Johnson, who never got to enjoy his fame. In his *Crossroad Blues* he wrote, "Tell my friend Willie Brown, that I got the crossroad blues this morning, Lord babe, I'm sinkin' down."

## The trembling earth

What are the odds of the casinos *sinking down*—that a second disaster could strike in the same place as the 1955 tornado? I'd bet the casinos would let you make a wager!

Some geologists say the odds are high, when you consider that the area is near the tail end of the New Madrid Fault, which runs roughly between Memphis and St. Louis. The area sits on a six-hundred-million-year-old pre-Cambrian rift that has been buried by sediment and is perhaps five miles below the surface.

In 1811 and 1812 the area was rocked for three months by earthquakes that were felt as far away as the Eastern Seaboard, causing church bells to ring in Boston. There was no Richter scale then, but scientists estimate it would have approached an eight on that seismometer, ten times greater than the 1989 quake in San Francisco!

The earth opened up and the Mississippi River actually flowed backward, forming new lakes, such as Reelfoot in Tennessee and Kentucky, and draining others. Huge "sand blows," geysers of waterborne sand, spewed up from the earth. One such site exists on our family farm and, because it was not suitable for agriculture, was designated as a graveyard site for farm families.

Because the earthquake epicenter area was so sparsely populated in the 1800s, the death toll was estimated to be in the hundreds, maybe five hundred. Today, such an upheaval could rival the force of hundreds of atom bombs, putting eleven million people at risk. It is projected that damages could exceed $200 billion.

Scientists estimate past upheavals have occurred in three-hundred- to five-hundred-year intervals. The clock is ticking. Head for the hills!

## The old ways vanish

The modern Delta is a far cry from the 1901 *Riparian* book's opening page, which has two photos. The first depicts a woodland hunt, with tents and men with guns and dogs. The caption says, "But for the disaster of overflows…fertile plantations would be here." A dead bear hangs from a tree.

The second photo is exactly the means to the end: a monstrous metal digging machine, showing dirt being piled up and molded into a section of the levee system.

The move to turn the responsibility for flood control over to the federal government, *Riparian* says, started in June 1890, in the midst of a huge overflow of the river, "to bring security to the homes of the people and to contribute to the development of the vast areas which were yet untrodden, almost, by the foot of man."

The Tunica and Chickasaw Indians most likely would have found this laughable, probably having trod or boated over every square mile of their former homelands in The Delta.

The highest point on the family farm (other than the levee) is an old Indian ceremonial/burial mound, which has been lowered over the years by constant overplowing. At first, when the plowman would unearth a grave, Granddaddy would be summoned.

Eventually the farmhands just plowed on through the graves. The mound is littered with bone fragments and pottery shards. When I was a boy I hunted in vain for a whole piece of Indian artistry, but all I could salvage were broken arrowheads and remnants of flint tools.

Some amateur archaeologists later dug around and removed intact pottery and skulls, but digging is now discouraged in the name of political correctness.

In his self-published book, *Tunica County—Scraps of History* (Xlibris, 2006), author-attorney John W. Dulaney Jr. says, "Our Indians had musical names such as Ish-to-ho-tapa, She-washa, Cha-wa, Mi-o-ta, and O-wah-lah-cush-tah. There was even one named Tat-too-tubby" (p. 16).

After the Indians were sent to Oklahoma in the early 1800s, he says, the US government had Tunica land surveyed and allotted into sections, townships, and ranges.

Tunica, which means "the people" in many Southeastern Native American languages, is named for an ancient migratory Indian tribe, which was decimated by diseases after de Soto showed up. In the 1600s the Chickasaws drove the Tunica Indians south into Louisiana, where the Tunica language died out when the last-known fluent speaker, Sesotrie Youchigant, died. The language became as long-gone as the later way of life that existed when I was growing up.

The Chickasaws, according to an article in *The Tunica Times* newspaper, "were deeply religious and were not superstitious, being unafraid of natural phenomena, unlike neighboring tribes. They believed that comets, eclipses and earthquakes were natural things made by and under the guidance of the 'Beloved One.'

"They declared that they believed in 'One who lived in the clear blue sky, and two with him, three in all,' and that they had known this always, as soon as the ground was sound and fit to stand upon."

## The death of the bear

It's ironic to me that the opening photos of the old *Riparian* book juxtapose the shot of dirt-moving equipment with that of a dead bear, since William Faulkner wrote about a bear that symbolized the rapidly vanishing way of life in Mississippi.

Although Faulkner's novella, *The Bear*, wasn't set in The Delta, it might as well have been. When I read this book in the ninth grade it had a life-changing effect on me because Faulkner was writing about *my* Mississippi.

I realized then that my life was rooted in a special place and time. In college, at Vanderbilt University, I majored in English, having gone through, and rejected, notions of pursuing medicine or the law.

Later, when Faulkner died on one of my birthdays, I grieved. His bear story still resonates with me.

In it, an old part-Negro, part-Indian guide decides to quit living when the old bear, having eluded hunters for years, is finally brought down.

Daddy was like the old bear: "...Jealous and proud enough of liberty and freedom to see it threatened not with fear nor even alarm but almost with joy…" One of the farm hands even called Daddy "Jack the Bear."

Daddy was certainly nearly as strong as a bear and was known for his ability to lift a twelve-inch wide cannonball up onto his shoulder. The cannonball had been discovered while farm workers were dredging sand along the river. It sits in my brother George's yard today, slowly sinking into the turf under its own massive weight.

## A big teddy bear

In a way Daddy was a big teddy bear, which is interesting since the doll by that name had its roots in the Mississippi Delta in 1902 when US President Theodore "Teddy" Roosevelt was taken on a bear hunt. He had come to join in political bargaining over a boundary dispute between Mississippi and Louisiana.

Trying to please the president, the Delta hunters wanted him to have the first kill. The dogs ran down a black bear cub, which was tied to a tree to provide an easy shot.

Summoned to the site, Roosevelt refused the shot, saying that it would be unsportsmanlike.

A political cartoon, entitled "Drawing the line in Mississippi," ran in *The Washington Post*, showing Roosevelt turning his back on a cuddly cub, which became known as "Teddy's Bear" and evolved into the famous child's doll.

## Gravity sucks

Daddy's mistress was the Delta dirt. It had a special effect on him, holding him there for eighty-eight years with a supernatural gravitational force. After marrying, he only went on very brief trips, preferring to stay home on his beloved land. When he died, The Delta simply sucked him into her bosom.

His farmland was broken into smaller parcels and I inherited about 220 acres. I sold it to my brothers. In a way I felt I was betraying my forebears, but my life is in Georgia now. Besides, my brothers are farming it and they have lots of grandchildren to pass it to. I only have one granddaughter, and she seems to be putting down her roots very well in Georgia.

When I visit my brothers and see all the keys they own, I wonder if their possessions own them.

I was riding in the car with Daddy one day, en route to Memphis, when we passed an old bum walking alongside the highway. "I'll bet he's happy," Daddy said with a tinge of envy. "He doesn't have a worry in the world."

My unspoken first reaction was a sarcastic, "Yeah, right!!!" Then it occurred to me that maybe this was his indirect way of condoning my wandering ways, of telling me he was envious of the year when I bummed, strummed, and thumbed my way around the world with a guitar and a backpack.

"Your daddy gave you wings," said a cousin later. "What a gift!"

Now, Daddy's worries are long gone, my wings are clipped, and the only land I own in Mississippi is a funeral plot.

It will own me some day.

**"THE STREETCAR TO DESIRE"**

*"Mammy" Perry*

*"Daddy" Perry*

*The Conductor*

*His Birthplace*

*Colonel Duke*

*On Vacation*

*The Home Place*

**GEORGE DAY PERRY**

*"JACK"* ~ *"THE CAP'N"* ~ *"DEAR"* ~ *"GRANDDADDY"*

# CHAPTER 4

## Way-back Jack

### When Jack met Sallie: a rags-to-riches romance

Why would anyone in his right mind fly from Atlanta, through smoke-darkened skies, into Orange County in southern California during the peak of the 2003 firestorm that was in the process of consuming some 600,000 California acres?

The answer: I was going to visit my ninety-year-old aunt, Elizabeth, the last survivor of nine children on my father's side of the family. We called her Aunt Ewee (pronounced *Eeee-wee*). I wanted to ask her about the family history.

It was the last time I saw Ewee; she died at the end of 2007, at ninety-four. The turnout for her Mississippi funeral was like a family reunion, not only because it was the end of an era, but because everyone loved her deeply.

Though bent sideways by scoliosis, Ewee had been a towering beacon to our entire family, a true lady of light who always looked for the best, never taking sides in family squabbles.

I was going into the darkness to soak up some of her special brand of California sunshine (she called me her "little boy" and even took me to Disneyland one last time) and to talk to her about the good old days.

There were dark old days, too, but Ewee could even find good in the fact that my great-grandfather, Francis "Frank" Jett Whitley, was some sort of Mason, Tennessee, dandy who squandered his family's farming fortune, perhaps as a riverboat gambler and perhaps simply by not adapting to the drastic changes brought on by the Reconstruction Era (also known, by some, as the Second Civil War).

## Frankly, my dear, I don't give a damn

"My Grandfather Frank had never learned to make money or even husband what resources he had, so his wealth trickled through his fingers," Ewee said.

As a youngster, his primary interest had been hunting and fishing. "He always had a young boy in attendance to saddle his horse, clean the fish and game, and open the gates so he never had to get down from his horse."

Eventually Frank went into a financial tailspin and ended up a traveling salesman, moving his wife and nine children to Memphis. "They took some rooms and his wife, my grandmother, nicknamed Totsie, took in sewing to help ends meet."

There was good in that, Ewee said, because their teenage daughter, Sallie, my grandmomma, "learned what it was like to really pinch pennies."

When a tenth Whitley child arrived, Totsie died of "child-bed fever" (really a broken heart, Sallie believed). The children were farmed out to relatives. Sallie, who was seventeen, took her two-year-old brother, Howard Whitley, as her own child and became a schoolteacher, living on a relative's farm.

"It was sad going back to Mason in need and want, where once they had walked so proud," said Ewee.

## Sallie draws a Jack

Enter George Day "Jack" Perry. As a stubborn teenager, he had fled the family's hardscrabble farm and a father who told him he wouldn't amount to much, to go his own way. He ended up working as a hired hand on the farm where Sallie had taken refuge with relatives.

"In her impoverished state and with a young child on her hands, Sallie didn't have too many suitors," said Ewee. "So she quickly took notice. Jack was hardworking and capable—and he made her laugh. He loved children."

Because Jack had started life in a dogtrot log house, Sallie's relatives advised her that his family was beneath her.

His family history is sketchy to me. His grandparents, Albert and Susan Perry, had moved from North Carolina to Wilson County, in middle Tennessee near Nashville, and later moved southwest to Adair, near Jackson, Tennessee, in 1832. Their seventh child, my great-grandfather Marshall, was only four when his forty-seven-year-old father died, leaving Susan with nine children to rear.

Marshall grew up and "outmarried" himself when he wed Sarah Priscilla Josephine Day, known as Mammy (who died in 1902 on the day my daddy was born). Although Marshall's prospects improved, he wasn't particularly well off. The couple had nine children, including my grandfather, George Day Perry, their fourth, nicknamed Jack after a family mule.

Sallie ignored her family's warnings and married Jack in 1897 at Trinity Episcopal Church in Mason, and moved with her infant brother, Howard, and Jack to nearby Memphis, where Jack had taken a job as conductor on a mule-drawn streetcar, known as a "dinky," for fourteen cents an hour.

I remember Miss Sallie telling me that Granddaddy had to get up for work at three a.m. on the day after the wedding: "The alarm went off and I sat bolt upright in bed, knowing that the whole town knew that there I was, *in bed with a man!*"

In Memphis, the couple began their own family with two sons, George Jr. and Frank. Following their mother's lead, the boys began calling their father Dear, adding another name to his repertoire.


## A streetcar to desire

The man named George, Jack, and Dear continued his work as a streetcar conductor until one day an old bachelor from Mason got on the streetcar and recognized him. The bachelor, Colonel B. F. "Tobe" Duke, was a pioneer in the Mississippi Delta. Levees were being built and he needed someone to clear more land and to manage his farm.

It seems that Colonel Duke was quite the ladies' man and looked a lot like Colonel Sanders of Kentucky Fried Chicken. The good women of Mason would always look down when they passed him on the street, pretending they didn't see him, said my aunt.

My grandparents were beyond worrying what "polite society" thought and in 1900 moved about forty miles south of Memphis to the Duke place, near Hollywood, in Tunica County, working for $350 a year.

"This was the hardest work they had ever done, but they liked it," said Ewee. "Jack was in the saddle from sunup to sundown, and Sallie was just as busy, keeping books and managing the house and gardens."

Still pinching pennies, Sallie began selling butter, eggs, and smoked hams in Memphis. She even sold pigeon squabs to the Peabody hotel, having acquired a breed of large "white king" pigeons from nephew Whitley Cox (who later ran against Jesse Owens in the Berlin Olympics tryouts, and lost, and then ran against an American quarter horse for one hundred yards, and won).

Sallie was quite bold, sometimes riding alone on the farm, sidesaddle on a horse, with a pistol strapped to her waist.

### The colonel makes a charge

My grandparents had such success that Colonel Duke thought that farming was easy and briefly tried to manage the farm himself.

Displaced, my grandfather moved his family to Cherry Valley, Arkansas, and worked with his brother, Marshall "Pete" Perry.

It wasn't long before the colonel figured out that he had bitten off more than he could chew, since he had only worked as a merchant before. He soon was begging Jack and Sallie to come back. They were glad to oblige.

They worked the place for twelve years, and when Colonel Duke died, he left the now-thriving farm to his two sisters, with instructions that if they sold, they should give Jack the first crack at buying. It wasn't long before they sold out to my grandparents.

### Miracle man hits the jackpot

As their brood grew to nine children, Jack and Sallie continued to prosper, buying more land every chance they got, including the

Johnson, Barton, and Drake places. Calling him a miracle man, the local newspaper noted that his holdings had grown to 16,800 acres in just fourteen years.

It may have grown to twenty thousand acres, counting woodlands and a brief flirtation with a grapefruit farm in Texas. It has been estimated that at one time he had 350 families working for him. He even briefly employed Sallie's father, Frank, as a farm manager.

Although Jack's children continued to call their father Dear in family situations, they began to refer to him outside of the family as The Cap'n. This was not a military title, but the title of captain commonly conferred on many planters by farm hands.

More than a farmer, he was a shrewd trader, said Tunica attorney John W. Dulaney Jr., who told me about the time his attorney father was attempting to close a land deal for Granddaddy. When the seller balked, Granddaddy simply raked the big stack of legal papers off the desk, in the direction of a trash can. "The man dove and caught the papers in midair," said Dulaney, noting that the deal sailed through without another hitch.


### Good dealers

The Cap'n and Miss Sallie were active Christians and were instrumental in founding Epiphany Episcopal Church in Tunica. "They established and nourished this church and, with little help, financed its construction and saw it consecrated in 1924," says attorney Dulaney in his book *Tunica County—Scraps of History* (p. 143).

The beautiful stained glass over the altar is dedicated to Granddaddy and a rear window is in memory of Miss Sallie.

For the farm families, they started plantation churches and schools. They despised the Ku Klux Klan and felt that "without an education the blacks didn't stand a chance," said Ewee.

Most Delta planters disliked the Klan, unlike some town merchants.

Turner Catledge, who worked for the local *Tunica Times* newspaper in 1922 and 1923, was prospering until the paper sided with the planters against the Klan, and many pro-Klan merchants pulled their advertising support. Catledge left and later became managing editor of the *New York Times*.

Even so, the Tunica paper "shamelessly propagandized the Negro about the joys of Tunica," he would write later, noting that the publication added "a colored column written by a crippled Negro who ran a pressing shop" to help persuade blacks to stay in the county.

## A child deals with vigilantes

I was almost a teenager before I finally came face-to-face with full-blown racism and found myself caught up in an angry mob of vigilantes.

This did not happen in The Delta. In fact, when asked, Daddy said he never knew of any lynching or vigilante activity in the area during his lifetime.

This idea was echoed in *Rising Tide*, John Barry's chronicle of the great Mississippi River flood of 1927. As background, the book details Delta planter Leroy Percy's 1922 stare down with the Klan, then a national power. My grandparents shared Percy's sense of obligation to their farm workers, which carried over to Daddy.

When Daddy died, we found a stack of letters written to him by former farm laborers who'd migrated up fabled Highway 61 to the "greener pastures" of factory jobs in Chicago and Detroit. The letters spoke fondly and nostalgically about the good old days on the farm.

Said one woman, "I write this because as we grow older sometime we wonder about our lives and how our living has affected others. Your kindness affected me. It caused me, when faced with racial problems, to remember there are some kind, thoughtful white people."

Maybe I was naïve, but as a child I had not known any other kind of white adults until that summer when, at about age twelve, I ventured with my mother to Lena, the Mississippi hamlet where her mother was living.

## A whole different game

Back then, Delta folks usually spoke of land outside The Delta as "the hills"—as if it were some foreign nation abutting the Delta flatlands. So there I was in this alien land. Shooed out of the house after lunch, I was bored stiff until I located another, older, boy down the road and struck up a game of basketball.

It was an early-summer afternoon and we were just working up a sweat when a procession of pickup trucks sped by. "Come on," my new friend yelled as he ran toward a nearby mercantile store. There, an angry mob, bristling with shotguns, was congregating. I had no clue what was happening and why these overall-clad men were so angry.

Within minutes men with bloodhounds arrived and soon I was jostling along in the back of a pickup, eating the dust of an armed convoy.

A few miles out of town, we stopped at the country home of a white woman. I overheard vague talk about her having been approached in a threatening manner by a black man.

The next stop was a shack where a black woman was being interrogated while her disabled, disfigured child sat on the porch, screaming in terror. It made me squirm, too.

The men passed through the house with the hounds. The mob followed on foot through fields and woods until the hounds stopped cold at the shore of a pond.

While the hounds circled the pond, trying to regain the scent, most of us headed for shade.

I was in the group that found its way into a collapsed underground tornado shelter or root cellar at an abandoned homesite. Sitting there quietly, I heard a squealing noise. I scratched through the rubble and found a pink newborn mouse. A huge black beetle had its pincers latched onto the mouse's leg.

## Of mice and men

To my surprise, one of the rough-looking young men in the group sensed my distress, grabbed the beetle, and, after setting the mouse free, gently released the beetle, too.

Whether the man we were chasing met the same compassion I'll never know, because I soon headed back to town with a truckload of posse dropouts.

Momma was concerned that I was late for supper, becoming mortified when I told her where I'd been. We had a very quiet meal.

No one ever told me how the chase ended, whether it involved Klansmen, or why they would treat a white boy like a man, letting him join the pursuit of a black man they thought of as a "boy."

When I arrived home the next day I was a lot older.

## Jackknives and candy

When I was much younger I would sometimes get to ride around the farm with my Granddaddy Jack. He always kept a box of candy by his side, to share with any children he might see. He also had a box of cheap jackknives, which he gave away much more selectively.

He loved to entertain the farm hands with snakes, trying to dispel their myths about serpents, including the hoop snake (which allegedly would bite its tail and roll toward you like a wheel) and the stinging snake (which allegedly would stick its head in the mud and sting you with its tail). If the snakes were nonpoisonous Granddaddy would let them go; if not, he'd kill them.

He would give his grandchildren silver dollars, which for some unknown reason he called Bo (or Beau?) Dollars, often used as a reward if you'd spend the night with him.

He had terrible hay fever and would go through a dozen handkerchiefs in a day, often draping them over furniture or church pews to let them dry. This practice got him expelled from a hotel lobby in California on a trip he made out west to visit his daughters.

When he sneezed, he let out a tremendous yell, presumably to bleed off some of the pressure in an effort to keep from expelling his brains through his nose. I inherited his hay fever, as well as my maternal grandmother's asthma.

## A giant folds his hand

When I was seven, Granddaddy died on June 23, 1949, at age seventy-nine, after going home one day for a nap on the sofa. (Ironically, this was Daddy's forty-seventh birthday, and Daddy was born on the day that Granddaddy's mother died.)

The day Grandaddy died, I was with Momma, who had taken Miss Sallie to shop in Memphis. On the way home, we saw a man standing beside a gravel road, frantically trying to wave us down with his handkerchief. Seeing that it was Dr. W. W. Nobles, our family doctor and longtime friend, we stopped.

Dr. Nobles strode grimly to Miss Sallie's side of the car and got right to the point. "He's gone," he said.

Grandmother took it with unbelievable stoicism, not shedding a single tear on the remaining trip home.

She kept the body on view at the family home for a couple of days as hundreds of mourners filed by to pay their respects.

One black man held his son up to the coffin. "He gave you candy," the man said.

In a eulogy to my grandfather in the 1949 "Colored News" section of the *Tunica Times,* black writer Joe Grant had this to say:

"He believed in education for colored people and would speak to them anywhere and any time... He believed in straightforward dealing in every way and the schools he built were quite a credit to the Perry Estate and a lasting benefit to our group... He was a man of broad vision... Sleep on, Mr. Perry, and take your rest. We loved you but God loved you best."

## A love note

Sallie lived on to age ninety-one. When she died, the family terrain began to move in seismological shifts.

Years later, when my younger brother, George, moved into our grandparents' home, a huge stack of family letters was removed from the attic and distributed among various family members. The only missive that I know of from Granddaddy is a love note dated March

30, 1926. He wrote:

"Sallie, This is a little remembrance of your 49 Birthday, & soon will be our 29 anniversary, which I will be in wedlock to you 27 years the 12 day of next May, that I must say I never have regreted. While this gift is nothing in compair to your companionship to me. While I am geting old & you are going to stay young, all I am going to ask of you, don't forget the one who loves you best. Dear."

A better indication of the depth of his love was evidenced in this story from Ewee, who was a young girl when Miss Sallie was in the Memphis hospital for "female troubles," presumably having a hysterectomy. "Dear telephoned to check on her and the doctor said, 'Oh, you know I told you she's not going to make it.'"

Ewee said she joined Dear in a long, sad car trip to Memphis. "He had to pull over and stop several times because he was sobbing so. Then, when we got to the hospital in Memphis, Dear quizzed the doctor, who apologized, 'Oh, I thought when you called you said you were Mr. *Terry* from *Tchula*!!!! Your wife's fine!' Dear was *so* relieved!"

Sallie was loved equally well by all of her family. As a child, I would slip across the road and visit her often, after stopping by the kitchen to get a big cathead biscuit from her rotund, jovial, gold-toothed mulatto cook, Miss Willie Pope, who would often recite poems to me, such as the one about the girl with a "squalid" (scarlet) cap who magically turned into a woodpecker.

I once asked grandmother what was the first thing Dear said to her. "That I was ugly," she laughed. To me, she was a duckling who had turned into a swan. She would be ensconced in her living room, surrounded by heavy ebony furniture that Dear had amassed from various estate sales. Most of the furniture was massive and had men's faces carved into the arms and legs, including about eighteen dining-room chairs needed to entertain her huge family. She looked regal to me.

"Totsie" Whitley

Raising Chickens & "Chillun"

"Frank" Whitley

A Sommerville Coat of Arms with dragon on top

Toby  Jack  Alex  Frank  George

Mary Jo

Virginia  Elizabeth  Clyde

## SALLIE JETT WHITLEY PERRY
*"MISS SALLIE" ~ "GRANDMOMMA" ~ "GRAM"*

# CHAPTER 5

## A Knight's Queen

### Descendant of a dragon slayer

Not only did Miss Sallie look like a queen on a throne, but she actually had some royal bloodlines—and other ancestors had rubbed elbows with royalty.

Her mother, Totsie, was a Somervell, descended from Sir Qualter de Sommerville (the spelling has changed numerous times). This Norman knight, whose name evolved from the Somme area of France, came to England in 1066 with William the Conqueror, who gave him baronies and estates.

His grandson, the second William de Sommerville, attained fame as a "dragon slayer." One account calls it "the last serpent in Scotland" and another calls it a "worm." I'm going with dragon. The details may be lost in the mists of time, but there is a creature depicted on the top of a Somervell coat of arms and it's the winged, fire-breathing dragon of our myths.

One thing is sure: the family continued to prosper. "Generations later," according one account, "John Somerville, in 1164, at fifteen years of age, went on a visit to Scotland. There King Malcolm IX of Scotland was pleased with the lad and made him a Page of Honor. Ten years later William the Lion knighted him Baron of Linton in Roxburgshire for great services to the country."

In 1297 his grandson, Walter, joined Sir William Wallace in the fight for Scottish freedom, commanding a cavalry brigade under Wallace at the Battle of Biggar. Wallace's exploits are depicted in the movie *Braveheart*, starring Mel Gibson.

"After generations, the family acquired estates and lived as Barons of Linton. Sir Thomas Somerville was made a lord in 1420, and was named Ambassador to London in 1425 to treat for the ransom and deliverance of James I of Scotland."

According to John Marshall, a distant cousin of mine, the Somerville barons "were on intimate terms with the Scottish kings and often hunted with them." They had colorful nicknames such as Velvet Eye, Red Bag, and Harrie Hot Spurres. One was a falconer for the king.

"However, by the 1600s the family's financial fortunes had declined to the point where they were no longer able to maintain their title," says Marshall.

James, the twenty-fourth in line from 1066, who spelled his name "Somervell," moved from Scotland to Maryland in the 1700s, possibly as a "factor" (agent) in the tobacco trade. Because he was not the eldest son in his family, he had not been in line to inherit the family estate. Still, he was able to amass a fortune through hard work.

His son, John II, moved to North Carolina, and one of his sons, John Somervell III, ended up with an estate in Virginia. John III's sons, including Richard "Dick" Bullock Somervell, Sallie's grandfather, migrated to Tennessee, settling in Mason in the early 1800s.

It was Richard's daughter, Mary Taylor "Totsie" Somervell, who married the hapless Frank Whitley. Later, when a yellow-fever epidemic swept through the area, her father, Dick, came to her garden, refusing to come in the house. He was ill and didn't want her to get sick. She visited with him from a distance in the garden, and then he left. She never saw him alive again. He was buried in a mass grave with other yellow-fever victims.

Sallie was one year old at that time. The way Sallie climbed out of poverty over the next ninety years, to become a genteel lady of grace, would have made the old Sommervilles proud.


### A genealogical genie

Sometimes, when you rub the lamp of history, a genie appears, as evidenced by the genealogical genie who flooded me with a wealth of additional information.

When I sent the text of this book to be checked for accuracy by Memphis attorney and West Tennessee historian John Marshall, a cousin whom I only recently discovered, he sent me more than three wishes' worth of colorful family history. My hat is off to him.

John provided the following journal notes, written in the late 1930s or early 1940s by Miss Sallie's Tennessee cousin, Clara Tarry, after she had visited the home of my grandparents, Jack and Sallie, near Hollywood, Mississippi, to attend a dance. The parenthetical notes are mine.

> We drove into the grounds of their fine home, on concrete, a line of garages, different make car for each member of the family. Lights, water and fans thro the house. Every variety of antiques, a room of books, large display of cut glass, two punch bowls, holding 2 gals, a buggy whip bought in Texas, ivory handle & gold band.

> Jack drove us over his plantation, earth black as the 'negroes' working, all wave at Jack, big cotton & corn, about to lay by, not a blade of grass. Drove on the Miss. river levee, took us to Moon [Mhoon] Landing, banks of concrete."

> [The concrete banks were made of concrete slabs wired together with steel cables and stretched over the bank like a blanket to keep the river's erosive powers at bay. This revetment work was installed and maintained by the US Army Corps of Engineers.]

> Jack works 1500 negroes, 500 mules, few riding horses, 15 trucks, has 100 hogs, 150 hams in his smoke house.

> He doesn't tell how much land he owns, but has five sons [six: perhaps one was omitted because he had left the farm], each with beautiful homes, daughters too. Sally [Sallie] has all sizes of fowls, even pea fowls…

> Their table groaned with goodies at noon. Sally's kitchen is large & attractive, every convenience. The cook's cottage is white,

furnished nice, with bath & lights. They have beautiful pictures with the Somervell Coat of Arms in color.

They have built a handsome brick church & rectory at Tunica. Their son gave the pipe organ. All their children, their sons & wives belong to the Episcopal & the babies, ten, are baptized.

They are a royal host & hostess. The display of silver looks like a jewelry store & Sally wears as many diamonds as a Queen, & she is a Queen.

[Note: Miss Sallie wore a huge diamond brooch, said to contain one large diamond for each of her nine children. I don't think it had that many stones, but I do know it was broken up at her death and the diamonds went to various heirs.]

Jack's farm bell cost $400, and is a tall belfry, like a church. They have a tennis court, with arc lights, a Doll house for the kiddies. The shrubs & flowers are lovely. The 'Cabins' [tenant houses] are painted white, in good repair, with nice fenced gardens.

Jack went to Florida last winter & met so many Yankees, told them when he reached home he was going to kiss every one of his negroes.

Jack's tenants own 40 automobiles. Jack's porch lights are the quaintest I ever saw, two at every door of his, & his children's home. They have a baby Grand piano & an imported violin, brought from 'over' the water near 100 years ago, by a relative.

## Big Daddy?

In 2008 I made a trip to Mason to visit with John Marshall, who took me and other relatives all over the Mason stomping grounds of our ancestors.

It was a fascinating, almost spiritual, experience—particularly when we were ushered into Trinity Episcopal Church where my grandparents were married in 1897. It is an architectural marvel, with beautiful, old stained-glass windows.

Because I had told John about the fact that Tennessee Williams had often visited my grandparents' Delta home, John asked if they might have served as a model in some way for the characters in the Tennessee Williams play *A Cat on a Hot Tin Roof.*

Intrigued, I later got a copy of the play and was relieved to find that the unflattering Big Daddy and Big Mama characters are poles apart from my grandparents. There are some similarities, though, even an old-maid relative named Miss Sally.

Tennessee Williams' Big Daddy Pollitt is a Mississippi redneck who quits school at age ten and goes to work in the Delta fields, gradually clawing his way up to farm overseer. He eventually comes to own a 28,000-acre plantation of "the richest land this side of the valley Nile."

Big Daddy comments on his greed, theorizing that his out-of-control buying sprees might stem from some irrational notion that one might be able to actually buy his way into eternity.

We used to joke that Granddaddy Jack only wanted the land that was next to his. He also enjoyed going to estate sales, buying often. His library was filled with leather-bound books signed by Memphis hotel owner John Gaston. I salvaged many of them, including some with dates in the 1700s, before they were to be thrown away.

Sometimes Granddaddy would ask his kids to stash his estate-sale purchases in their homes, so Miss Sallie wouldn't find out what he had bought. I have a few of the pieces in my home, as do many of my cousins.

I must say he had a good eye for bargains. One of my cousins, Jo Cochran of Memphis, was given one of these items, a vase, by an aunt. Jo recently took the vase to be appraised on the *Antiques Roadshow* television program and her mouth dropped open when it was valued at $10,000.

## More real-life characters

John Marshall was able to provide some more details on my ancestors and other characters.

He said that Totsie's father, my great-great grandfather Richard "Dick" Somervell, was nine when his mother died and eleven when his father passed away on the family plantation in Virginia. Here, with John's permission, is his account:

"Dick's father, in his will, left 'his negro woman Bettie' to Dick. The will specifically requested that Bettie be made comfortable and pretty much given whatever she wanted. She was only about thirty at the time and pregnant, to boot. This makes me wonder if she was the Sallie Hemings (Thomas Jefferson's alleged mistress) of our family. She later came to West Tennessee with the Somervells and was confirmed as the first black member of Old Trinity Episcopal Church in Mason.

"I imagine Bettie reared Dick and his younger brother, Bob, who was said to be a little tetched in the head. Supposedly, when still just an infant, Bob had fallen out of the horse-drawn carriage and the wheel ran over his head, thus causing his affliction. One of the older Somervell brothers later became a Methodist preacher, and some in the family would later joke that perhaps the carriage wheel had run over *his* head instead.

"Bob lived to about forty-six, never married, and divided his time between his brothers' plantations. Always a spiffy dresser, he was often seen driving through the neighborhood with a pretty team of horses, his valet at his side. While the census listed the occupations of his brothers as attorney, planter, and minister, Bob simply was listed as a hunter."

## The brightest brother

John continued: "When Dick's older brothers moved to the Mason area of Tennessee, young Bob and Dick, a teenager by then, came with them. Dick was probably the brightest of the brothers. They sent him to Nashville to school and then on to the University of Virginia where he graduated in law in 1841. He returned to Mason and started purchasing land near his brothers.

"In 1847 he married a sixteen-year-old cousin, Virginia Taylor. Their grandfathers were brothers and both were colonels in the American Revolution. The marriage was an advantageous one. Her father had just died and left her about thirty slaves and six hundred acres of land, called Scrub Oak.

"Virginia died four years later and Dick, with a small son and daughter now, next married Virginia's first cousin, Bettie Hunt, who was *also* his cousin, two times over."

## Shades of *Gone With the Wind*

"The Somervells," John said, "were kind of like the Wilkes family in *Gone With the Wind*, in that they preferred to marry within their own bloodlines. You know Ashley first rejected Scarlett O'Hara so he could marry Melanie, who was his cousin. Ashley wasn't joking when he told Scarlett he needed to 'marry his own kind!'

"I would say the Whitleys were a little more like the O'Haras.

"Bettie Hunt's family was among the last to come to the area from back East, and her father, Major Hunt, was an elegant gentleman and fine hunter—who already had gone through five fortunes.

"Dick would soon follow suit. Before the Civil War, he had practiced law and farmed, living in a home called Royal Oaks, with six thousand acres, much of it woodland in the Hatchie bottoms. He also had a home in Memphis and was elected to represent Tipton and Shelby counties in the state legislature. Although I don't think he ever served in the military, like many Southern planters of the day he became known as 'Colonel' Somervell.

"Early during the war, Bettie died, leaving him with four more small children, including young Totsie."

## The bigger they are, the harder they fall

John continued, "It could be argued that Dick, the most successful Somervell brother, fell the hardest after the war. As administrator of the estate of his oldest brother, he was accused of 'getting funny with the money,' which resulted in all sorts of internecine litigation. Relatives said his family wanted to 'entertain in style and fly high'—which ruined him financially.

"Oral tradition says that when he died in the infamous yellow-fever epidemic of 1878, he was buried in a hasty mass grave behind where the Mason water tower is now. However, there is a marker for him at the Old Trinity Church, probably placed there by Dear and Miss Sallie at a later date.

"In my youth I played among the oaks at Royal Oaks. There were pastures, orchards, barns, and many other outbuildings, mostly gone now, victims of modern farming, which dictates that every available inch of land be devoted to row crops.

"The old house burned in 1899, just six years after Miss Sallie's family moved away, but a big patch of buttercups survived. I'm sure Miss Sallie must have picked some of those flowers in her childhood.

"The site is just a few miles away from Red Bud, the Whitley home where Frank's family lived. Frank didn't get this property, since it went to a sister, so he and Totsie ended up with Royal Oaks after Colonel Somervell, who had lost the place, somehow got it titled in Frank's name. At that time, with Reconstruction causing chaos, they were just trying to stay a step ahead of their creditors."

## Too light for heavy work

"Basically," John added, "the main problem was that many men of these old families were 'too light for heavy work and too heavy for light work,' to borrow a phrase from a cousin. Some of them had big appetites and were said to be 'digging their graves with their teeth.'

"Miss Sallie's father, Frank Whitley, was no different from his peers on the old plantations around Mason and in fact 'kept things together' better than some.

"Having been raised in luxury, many of the sons of wealthy planters were not accustomed to hard physical labor and felt it was beneath them. Additionally, they had been deprived of the management experience possessed by the previous generation. The results were disastrous, and many had to go into town for clerking jobs or survive by gradually selling off small tracts of land."

The too-light label did not apply to my Granddaddy Jack Perry, who really wasn't afraid to roll up his sleeves and work. Said John, "He was in some ways like Miss Sallie's grandfather, Captain Daniel R. Whitley, who also became a man of substance with no aristocratic background.

"Captain Whitley came to Tipton County about 1831 with a dozen or so slaves and bought one thousand acres. At his death, twenty-five years later, his holdings had grown to about nine thousand acres and 172 slaves.

"Captain Whitley's wife, Sallie Jett, was from a more genteel background and an Episcopalian, both of which had a powerful effect, I'm sure, on their granddaughter, Sallie Jett Whitley, as far as founding the church in Tunica and supporting schools for the farm hands.

"Since the older Perry family eventually bought about two hundred acres of the Red Bud property, the Perry and Whitley families would have been acquainted, but I'm sure that the Whitleys felt that young George Day 'Jack' Perry was 'beneath' Sallie Jett Whitley. Thank goodness she had better judgment!"

Amen to that!

The Nine Siblings left to right: Andrew, Ollie, Myra, Vardaman, Mable, Gretchen, Georgia, Bracie, Kate

George Washington Pace & Laura McKee Pace

Georgia

## GEORGIA PACE PERRY
*"The Madame" ~ "Momma" ~ Mamaw"*

# CHAPTER 6

## Georgia Pace Draws an Ace

### Momma's warring family of peace

Georgia, my Momma, was tough. She had to be, since most of her ancestors were of fairly modest means. As best I can tell, they were all pretty scrappy.

Her surname was Pace, a Welsh name that evolved from the Easter-related Latin word *pacha* and came to be spelled *pace,* as the Italians spell their version of the word for peace. They weren't all peaceful.

There was a Richard Pace of note who settled in 1620 at Pace's Paines (fields) near Jamestown, after he and his wife Isabella were each given one hundred acres of land just for showing up. According to a Virginia historical marker, "On the night before the Indian massacre of March 22, 1622, an Indian, Chanco, revealed the plot to Pace, who reached Jamestown in time to save the settlers in that vicinity." More than three hundred settlers were killed.

The Paces, their son, George Pace, and the Indian boy, Chanco, whom they'd taken in to live with them as a son, survived. A few years later Pace was killed while on an Indian raid and his widow, Isabella, married another settler, mariner Captain William Perry, likely creating the first Perry-Pace union in America.

We'd like to claim them all as ancestors, even though Isabella Perry is reported to have testified in a witchcraft trial, but no luck so far. (By some accounts Isabella was a sister or cousin of Captain John Smith.)

Momma's great-great-grandfather, Frederick Pace, came to America from Wales in 1768 with his wife, Elizabeth (nee Jones), and six children, one of whom later served in the Revolutionary War.

The family left South Carolina about 1800 and moved to Tennessee. They next tried Kentucky and, in 1809, traveling with a group of families with sixty pack horses, they settled in the Mississippi

Territory before the territory was split into two states, Alabama and Mississippi.

In 1811 my great-great-grandfather, Thomas Jefferson Pace, was born. He married a girl with the intriguing name of Jincy Ann Touchstone. They farmed and had twelve children.

When the Civil War broke out, Thomas organized a citizens company of more than fifty men, of which he was elected captain. Although the unit served "without cost" to the Confederacy, Thomas paid a high price: two of his sons were killed in battle.

My great-grandfather, James R. Pace, survived the war, even though he was shot in the foot once and was captured, paroled, and recaptured.

He later married Mildred J. Mathis and settled on one thousand acres (two hundred in cultivation) in Newton County, Mississippi, where he was elected to the board of supervisors, served as school commissioner, and served a four-year term in the state legislature.

The ninth of his eleven children was my grandfather, George Washington Pace, who married Laura McKee. They farmed in a succession of very small, middle-Mississippi towns and had nine children. One son, Andrew, was gassed in World War I, but survived.

George Washington Pace was a stern man, according to one of his sons, who said he often got thrashed way too long after he had outgrown the spanking stage. "I finally told him he wasn't going to whip me any more and left home for good," he said.

Daughter Bracie said the only time she saw her daddy cry was when she was a little girl and he asked her to hold a jack in place while jacking up their house. The jack slipped and crushed the tips of several of her fingers, she said. (She later regained use of the crushed fingers.)

In his old age, Granddaddy Pace asked if he and Laura could move in with the family of Ollie, a son living in Lena, Mississippi, who accommodated him. Granddaddy died shortly thereafter of a stroke and heart attack, at age seventy-two, leaving the family to theorize that he knew the end was near and wanted Laura taken care of.

An extreme asthmatic, Laura was emaciated and appeared to be on death's door, but lived another fifteen years. She was a shadow of her former self, when she could play a fiddle and dance a jig.

## Fleeing from Ireland

I once sat Momma down in front of a video camera and started quizzing her about the family history, but she soon begged out of the exercise, after telling me about the family's team of white horses, Old Rube and Dixie, and about her maternal grandfather, John McKee, a little Irishman who kept a bag of gold coins under his bed.

I know very little about Momma's ancestral history. My cousin, Ouda Shellyn Pace Gresham, says that Laura's father fled Ireland during the famine of the mid 1800s.

"Because of the potato blight," she says, "John McKee...came with his mother, brother, and sister to the New World. It has been suggested that there was not enough money for his father to come."

They landed in Boston and the brothers set off to find land to farm, telling their mother and sister that they would return for them later. After finding land in Mississippi, at least one of them returned to Boston but could find no trace of their mother and sister, whom the brothers never saw again.

Back in Mississippi, John married Margaret Emily Kelly. Their ninth child was Laura, my grandmother.

After she was widowed, Laura would often visit with her nine children and their families. "She'd stay a few days, then want to go home," said Bracie. "She stayed the longest with Georgia."

I can remember Grandmother Pace visiting with us, often sitting quietly, crocheting gifts for her family and gasping for breath. She also could sew beautiful dresses and didn't need patterns to do it.

A snuff dipper, she always had a spit cup at the ready. It is said she started dipping at sixteen, when snuff had been prescribed to ease a toothache.

Cousin Ouda says Grandmother Pace loved to sit and hold her grandbabies, watching soap operas on television. However, as soon as a wrestling program came on, she was quick to relinquish the tots. "She would sit on the edge of her chair and throw as many or more punches as the ones who were wrestling. Her favorite wrestler was Gorgeous George."

I think Laura had simply caught the Pace fighting spirit. She certainly gave Father Time a good wrestling match. Peace came to her at age eighty-five.

I inherited her asthma and can remember endless childhood nights, sitting up in bed, fighting for breath, longing to hear the rooster crow. This would tell me that Daddy would soon be getting up. He would boil a hypodermic needle and give me a shot of adrenaline, which would speed up my heart enough for the little oxygen in my lungs to get into my bloodstream.

Then, for a few hours, my fighting would be done. I would slip into a state of bliss, a state of peace. *Pace*.


## "The Madman"

Daddy always referred to Momma as the madame, in spite of a note he had from a maid who was relaying to him instructions from "The Madman." (He kept this with the cook's note that said, "The *fool* is in the oven.")

Far from mad, Momma was about as steady as a dry-docked ship. She came into this world in 1912, the same year the Titanic made its ill-fated maiden voyage, and for eighty-nine years she was unsinkable.

Christened Georgia Odell Pace, she was the seventh of nine children (six girls and three boys, just the opposite of Daddy's family of six boys and three girls). Her parents farmed a few acres near Union, Mississippi, and later moved to Sebastopol, in central Mississippi, where Momma attended school.

They were so poor, Momma said, that when the Great Depression hit, "We didn't even notice any difference."

She may have grown up *poor*, but her grandson Jack (my son, who was born on her birthday) said at her funeral that she was actually *pure*.

The only thing we know she ever did wrong, my brother Duke said, was when she was a girl and her father was milling sorghum. She earned a spanking when, for some unknown reason, she decided to stick her toe in the molasses. We think she just wanted to be a little sweeter.

Granddaughter Perry Eaton Hatch did admit that Momma encouraged her to drive over the speed limit while Perry was being taught to drive. This was on the way home from shopping trips to Memphis, where Momma would buy groceries and knickknacks—such as a *huge* brass eagle—that she would smuggle into the house in a game of cat and mouse, hoping Daddy wouldn't notice what new thing she had bought.

My wife, Penny, learned many of her wonderful mothering skills from Momma, after watching her throw her arms around her family members with big warm hugs. When the grandchildren started coming, Momma's name evolved into Mamaw.

As a teenager, Momma had dropped out of high school for a year to devote herself to her sick, asthmatic mother. And when her only daughter, her beloved Jett, lingered for months in the hospital, dying of cancer at the age of twenty-nine, Momma was constantly by her side with a steady presence that was true and unflinching.

## The turn

It was probably this quiet strength that attracted Daddy, a thirty-five-year-old bachelor, to Momma, who was twenty-five and working as a hatcheck girl in Memphis at the Peabody, where Daddy spent lots of weekends partying.

Daddy was as wild as he was handsome, I'm advised by numerous sources. Once, he was almost banned from the Peabody when his brother, Toby, let a live snake loose in the lobby. Daddy confirmed this tale, along with the story of being arrested for having a flask of alcohol in his coat pocket during Prohibition.

"Clyde [another brother] was already in jail, and when he saw me coming he said, 'You've come to get me out!' I said, 'Naw, move over.'"

There were other accounts, which he wouldn't confirm, such as crashing a car into a display window of Goldsmith's, a Memphis department store.

However wild he was, by all accounts he did a 180-degree turn when he met Momma and put the alcohol away forever, except for an occasional glass of wine—which every now and then included "vodka wine." (He insisted that vodka is indeed a wine, once telling a brother,

"Yeah it is! *It's from the Ukraine, monkey!*"—and that has become a family-reunion mantra.)

As evidence of Daddy's turnaround, on one of their first dates he took Momma to see the new blockbuster movie *Snow White.* Momma, I'm sure, felt that at last her prince had come.

"The lady who introduced us told me he was a fine man from a fine family and she was right," said Momma. The feeling was mutual; in a letter, Daddy referred to Momma and her family as "the salt of the earth."

## A 5:00 a.m. wedding

The year was 1938. An average three-bedroom home cost $3,900. The average income was $1,996. Jefferson's image replaced the Indian head on the nickel. Orson Welles' radio program, *The War of the Worlds,* scared the nation. Popular songs included *My Heart Belongs to Daddy* and *September Song.*

The most momentous event, for me, was my parents' wedding at 5:00 a.m. on September 1, in Epiphany Episcopal Church, the church founded by Daddy's parents. The Rev. Walter Dakin, grandfather of famed playwright Tennessee Williams, performed the service, with my paternal grandparents and a few members on hand, including mother's Memphis sisters, Bracie and Gretchen.

Why 5:00 a.m.? "Jack didn't want a crowd," Momma said. "He said we had a long way to go and a lot to do." They drove to Chicago, arriving before dark, and had a weeklong honeymoon in the Windy City.

## Hollywood housewife

Then it was home to the farm near Hollywood, Mississippi, where Momma threw herself into housewifery with enthusiasm and soon gave birth to Sallie Jett Perry, who was named after Miss Sallie. She was known as Jett, never got a nickname, and was a tremendous little athlete. She is survived by two daughters.

I came next, nearly two years later. I was named after nobody (J), and got my paternal grandmother's maiden surname (Whitley); I often have to write my name as "J (initial only) Whitley 'Whit' Perry." Various family members call me Whitticus or J Wellington (after a cartoon character, J. Wellington Wimpy) or J Wellington Whitehead. I answer to all.

Next came George Pace Perry, who was named after both grandfathers and got stuck with being called George Pace, which evolved into Georgie Porgie, then Porge, then Wild Man, then simply Wild. He's not so wild today, riding herd on vast farmlands and the fourteen grandchildren his five children have produced.

George is only fourteen months younger than I. Because I was asthmatic and small for my age, we were usually about the same size. We got into so many fights (all provoked by George, of course) that Daddy finally gave up and bought boxing gloves so we could duke it out.

Then came the real duke, Duke Hayley Perry. Born quite a few years later, Duke was named after his Uncle Toby *Duke* Perry (who himself was named after old man Duke, who gave Granddaddy his start in The Delta). Hayley came from Daddy's profligate college chum, George *Hayley*.

Daddy called Duke Mannish Thang (borrowing from the blacks' tradition of labeling a cocky young boy as mannish). Today he's the Duke of The Delta and presides over his own farming operation. His three daughters are providing him with lots of grandchildren.

For Momma, rearing her four children was a full-time job. She occasionally had to resort to stripping a privet-hedge limb and switching us—when she could catch us.

Daddy was equally elusive. During farming season he worked from sunup to sundown. Then came hunting season, when he usually would get up and head out before first light.

## A bird in a gilded cage

This left Momma with a lot of time to herself. She didn't really mesh well with some of her sisters-in-law, particularly one who, Daddy said, had snobbishly "high-hatted" her.

Sometimes I'd catch Momma staring wistfully out a window, like a bird in a gilded cage.

Still, she bucked up and was always true and loyal to Daddy.

She seemed to bask in the affections of the sales ladies in the fashion houses of Memphis, perhaps going overboard with clothing purchases. I know this because I had to go with her a lot, to get allergy shots in Memphis.

I quickly got bored with the faux fawning of the fashion mavens and more than once had to be scolded, particularly for running up the down escalator at Goldsmith's.

A telling letter in the files, from Momma to Daddy, says, "Please accept my humble apologies if I seem ungrateful for all the wonderful things you give me in the way of fur, jewelry, clothes and most of all your wonderful love. For you are truly the most wonderful husband a girl ever had…You are the one I want to look nice for."

She lived for a decade after Daddy died, eventually succumbing at eighty-nine to an infection, perhaps related to the diabetes which she had developed in her sixties. For the last few years of her life she was bedridden, cared for by a couple of wonderful black ladies who seemed to really love Momma. "We'll stay with her," one told me, "until death do us part." They did.

Momma's last words were "Mama, Papa, Bracie [a sister]." As ever, she was thinking about family. She left a note saying, "I want you all to live in peace and harmony and to bring up the grandchildren to love one another, for my sake."

## A hoard of memories

Rummaging through her cabinets after her death, we found that Momma had kept almost everything. There were boxes of letters and photographs. In one envelope we found many of her love letters from Daddy.

Most of the love letters are anniversary notes dated "Five o'clock in the morning, Sept. 1." I can see Daddy now, scribbling away before heading out the door for work. I bet he wrote fifty-two of them, although I can't find that many.

Some were short and sweet, such as "Sugar 'n the mornin, sugar 'n the ev'nin, sugar at suppertime. You are all the sugar I need all the time...I am on a diet...Your sugar, too."

Others were more serious, such as, "I don't know what I would have done without you, it is the best decision I ever could have made...I love you with all my heart." Or, "I never let a night pass that I don't express my thanks to God that I have you by my side." And, "A faithful and true wife...I could not ask for anything more."

Even the envelopes had messages. On some he drew the stamps and postmarks. One "stamp" shows Uncle Sam saying, "Watch out. I got my eye on you!"

On the first day of every September I think of them and the song they would sing together on that day: "I'll always remember that golden September, sweet cider time when you were mine."

Alex
George   Frank
Jack

STAR

**Jack Whitley Perry**
"The combined qualities of a gentleman and a
great athlete."
Varsity Football 1920-21; Varsity Basketball
1920-21; Varsity Baseball 1920-21; Vice-President Pierian Literary Society 1920; President
1921; Y. M. C. A. 1920-21; Vice-President
1921; Pocket Testament League 1920-21; Vice-
President Senior Class 1921; President of
Senate 1921.

### PERRY & NUTT
VENTRILOQUISTS
Lessons $1.50 a week—Work Guaranteed
Learn to Throw Your Voice 150 Feet

*Jack, second from right, with parents and siblings.*

# JACK WHITLEY PERRY
## "SON" ~ "BELLY" ~ "DADDY" ~ "PAPAW"

# CHAPTER 7

## The Ace

### A hunter-farmer who knew how to laugh

Daddy was a simple man—a basic hunter-farmer. It was said he was his mother's favorite, because he made her laugh. He never lost his zest for life. He was hard of hearing, probably deafened by too many gunshots, and wasn't much on making the social rounds. He could be graceful, but gags ruled his social life since he couldn't hear well enough for easy conversation.

He married at thirty-six and died at eighty-eight, still trying his best to make us laugh. As he lay dying, he stuck out his hand to me, as if to shake hands. Then he began trying to thumb wrestle with me, having fun until the last. He jokingly asked me to get in bed with him, and later suggested we try to make a getaway, saying weakly, "Open the door and let's go!"

He knew he was done for, stoically asking a strange visitor, "You come for my tombstone?" A plaque in the hall of the hospital, presumably placed there during a fund-raising drive, indicated he was in the "George D. Perry Room."

I'm glad Daddy died in his Daddy's hospital room in The Delta, the place he never wanted to leave, because the land—the farm, the woods, and the levee that divided them—was Daddy's mistress. He reveled in the place. He simply called his home "The Place," nothing fancy.

### A Hollywood story

Just how Daddy and his eight siblings survived childhood is nothing short of miraculous.

The settlement nearest to the family farm was Hollywood, about a mile away, across McKinney Bayou, near a grove of holly trees, from whence the name came. A railroad town, Hollywood featured a little railroad station, a sawmill, a cotton gin, a small hotel for salesmen (known as drummers), a few stores, and a variety of houses.

There's some great information on Hollywood in the July/August 1967 issue of *The Delta Review*, a now-defunct magazine once published by William King Self (quoted here with the permission of William King Self Jr., co-trustee of the Self Foundation).

In an article titled "Mud, Mules and Molasses" (pp. 30-100), Dr. Henry B. Gotten shed much light on hardships, stating that the primitive conditions he found growing up in Hollywood "were common to all inhabitants of this area, regardless of their race, social or economic conditions."

Dr. Gotten attended classes in Hollywood with Daddy and about sixteen other white students, grades one through ten, in an unpainted one-room schoolhouse with two outhouses, located in a field at the end of a dirt road, which often was so muddy that students arrived with "great balls of mud" accumulated on their shoes.

The drainage ditches along the road "provided good sport for we could wade, hunt for frogs or make mud balls" during recess, he said.

Students brought their own lunches, often eating outside, he wrote. "Once in a while we would 'spread' which meant that everyone put his lunch out in picnic style and you could 'go for grabs.' We all survived with no evidence of malnutrition."

Classes included "mental arithmetic" and recitations, with each student working at his or her own pace. "Primitive though the school was, somehow we absorbed enough to make our grades in the schools into which we later transferred."

Dr. Gotten lived in Hollywood when most houses had no screens. Some Deltans have noted that the screen was one of the greatest inventions ever. My grandparents certainly thought so and eventually had a screen porch that was hundreds of feet long, almost entirely surrounding their home.

## An unhealthy proposition

Wrote Dr. Gotten, "To say that The Delta was an unhealthy area is an understatement of the first order. Flies and mosquitoes in swarms were accepted as were chills and fever, accepted and endured."

Mosquitoes were fought with smoke buckets and mosquito bars (suspended nets that hung over beds). Outhouses near the houses' shallow-well pumps added to the medical maladies, which ranged from malaria to a "walking disease" known as yellow jaundice (later known as viral hepatitis). Croup and boils (later identified as staph) were common.

Treatments included calomel (which caused mild mercury poisoning), Epsom salts, quinine, and chill tonic, he said.

"It is said that the people of Mississippi believed in quinine, calomel and white supremacy," Dr. Gotten wrote. "A dose of calomel was given everyone who was sluggish or constipated or who thought his liver needed a good workout."

Other treatments included fat-meat and bread poultices, mustard plasters, and necklaces made of stockings that were soaked in coal oil (kerosene), turpentine, and lard. Laudanum was used for pain.

"It was said if you were sent to the hospital you were not expected to recover, and usually you did not," he wrote.

(My uncle Toby defied the odds when his appendix ruptured and he barely made it alive, by train, to a Memphis hospital. My uncle Alex survived with a home remedy when, as a baby, he began wasting away. "They found out that he liked sardines," Daddy said, "so they just kept feeding them to him until he got well. I think that close call made him the Cap'n's favorite.")

## Trains and riverboats

The train was a lifeline and its tracks were built up high enough to keep it chugging along even if a flood occurred. When the tracks were abandoned recently, local farmers were able to buy many truckloads of gravel from the railroad company.

Dr. Gotten said there were two trains to and from Memphis that passed through Hollywood: the cannonball, which stopped in Tunica and Clarksdale, and the accommodation, which made all the stops, including Hollywood. Its small, unpainted depot was home to a local stationmaster who lived upstairs with his family.

Trains competed with steamboats, which still plied the Mississippi River. Dr. Gotten wrote that boats to Memphis were often shared with rental mules, which were sent to higher ground after the farming season ended.

"We boarded the boat at Leatherman's landing," he wrote. "Every second was exciting, sitting on the upper deck watching the river, listening to the deep blasts of the whistles, eating on board with white covered tables and white-uniformed waiters and finally sleeping in a bunk. When we awakened we were in Memphis at the foot of Jefferson Avenue. Life was indeed worthwhile."

He said law and order in Hollywood was not a problem, even though the nearest law-enforcement officer was in Tunica, five miles away.

There were about twenty-five white families and hundreds of black families living in the town. "Every white man carried a pistol and no Negro was to be caught with one," he said.

"Difficulties were unusual except for fights between Negroes on Saturday night," he said, noting that justice was meted out with a certain practicality to accommodate the planters, with guilty parties sometimes "returned to their crops," as though that was punishment enough.

## The gentleman jock

When they outgrew the Hollywood school, Dr. Gotten moved with his family, leaving The Delta for the Mississippi hill city of Oxford. Daddy attended the agricultural high school in Tunica, where students stayed in a dormitory.

For his last two years of high school, Daddy was sent off to McCallie School for boys in Chattanooga, Tennessee, where his senior yearbook portrait has this caption: "The combined qualities of a gentleman and a great athlete."

The rest of the copy states: "McCallie takes pride in her graduates. There are, however, some who stand out, some of whom McCallie is justly more proud of than others… Such a man is Jack Perry. Since his entrance two years ago, Jack has helped every movement of good along with unlimited energy."

It glows with praise for his abilities as a football back, a basketball center, and a baseball pitcher, and praises his leadership abilities: "The respect that he commands from the student body was shown when they elected him Senator-at-large and also President of the Senate, one of the highest honors a boy can hold." He was also vice president of the senior class.

One of Daddy's great regrets was the school's last-minute decision to not give him a coveted school medal at graduation. This was because the underclassmen under Daddy's care tore out a dorm wall the night before. Daddy kept a photo of the damaged wall, having written on it, "This cost me the Grayson Medal."

## How to "throw" your voice

He also got into trouble with an enterprise that earned him praise in his senior yearbook: "He is a great ventriloquist, his ability to make inanimate things speak having startled many of us." There is an ad in the back of the annual for "Perry & Nutt—Ventriloquists. Lessons $1.50 a week—Work Guaranteed. Learn to Throw Your Voice 150 feet."

This, as it turned out, was a scam. Abetted by Robert "Boob" Nutt, Daddy would work his mouth during the lessons and Boob would be hidden away somewhere, awaiting his cue: "Okay, I'm going to throw my voice!" This would be followed by some closed-mouthed gyrations of the voice thrower's face muscles. A far-off voice would then say something such as, "Mama, I want some peanuts." They would take turns "teaching."

All the tuition money they had collected had to be returned when one of them accidentally stepped between the attic rafters one day, shoving his foot through the dormitory ceiling.

Boob went on to make a fortune with a memory-building book.

Years later, his son Buck Nutt blew into LaGrange, Georgia, where I now live, and persuaded the LaGrange Rotary Club to sponsor his memory-building course. He was astounding, naming all one hundred-plus Rotarians whom he'd just met a few minutes before.

Like some latter-day Music Man he presented his seminar and left town with thousands of dollars, having made help-me-and-I'll-help-you promises to various Rotarians—which he didn't keep, later canceling the life insurance policy which he'd "bought" and canceling delivery on the Buick he'd "ordered."

## Jack Son

Daddy evolved into a man of utter honesty. He just wasn't cut out to be a minister, a profession his mother hoped he'd pursue when he entered the University of the South (Sewanee), in the mountains of southeastern Tennessee.

Back then, Sewanee was a football powerhouse. For example, the 1899 team traveled 2,500 miles in five days and shut out five teams—Texas, Texas A&M, Tulane, LSU, and Ole Miss!

At Sewanee, Daddy "majored" in football. He was a star end and played offense and defense, once bragging that he had tackled a man named Johnny Mack Brown, who later became a movie star in western oaters.

Daddy certainly didn't focus on scholastics. For example, although he studied Spanish at Sewanee, the only phrase he could muster was, "*Los Estados Unidos compra vive usted amigos.*" It means "The United States buys lives [as in he *lives* somewhere] you friends." He enjoyed impressing people with his "fluency."

He later explained that the Spanish professor was nearly blind and there were lots of students willing to throw their voices for the benefit of football players when they were called on to recite Spanish phrases.

Daddy also majored in fraternity parties, joining Kappa Alpha. His best friend, during and after college, was Memphian George Hayley—known as Country Fool, which later got shortened to CF after Momma complained that whosoever calleth a man a fool is in danger of hellfire.

On football trips Daddy would smuggle CF onto the team's train, where the interloper would scurry under the seats to avoid detection.

They partied together and once entered a costume-party contest, dressing as an "overgrown country boy," with CF in a long overcoat and riding on Daddy's shoulders. Daddy said he got so hot and dizzy under the coat, dancing with girl after girl, that he finally puked. They still won top prize.

(Daddy's partying carried over to his bachelor farming days, but he said he often carried a big alarm clock strapped to his belt, so he could leave early enough to be at work before sunup the next day.)

After three years of fun, Daddy headed back to the family farm without earning a degree.

What he did earn was the nickname Son, a term he used to taunt upperclassmen his freshman year because football players were immune from hazing. Daddy didn't know immunity ended at the end of football season!

I can hear the upperclassmen now: "How do you like *that*, **SON**!?!" Whap!


## Down to business

After studying bookkeeping for a year in New Orleans, Daddy spent the next fifteen years as a professional hunter-farmer bachelor, with occasional weekend revelries in nearby Memphis, where he often partied at the Peabody—until he met "the prettiest girl in the world."

After marriage, Daddy settled down, eventually inheriting about seven hundred acres of flat Delta farmland alongside the Mississippi River levee. He called it simply "The Place." He was content with it. It was his kingdom. Except for adding eighty acres, he saw no reason to try to expand.

He also saw no reason to leave the farm. "The only thing I know of that Jack ever did wrong was refuse to travel with Georgia," said Aunt Bracie, Momma's sister.

His playground was "The Woods"—several hundred acres he

owned "across the levee," where he generously hung "Posted" signs to discourage unauthorized hunting. When the weather didn't permit farming, it was time to hunt—and, whether he was hunting game or poachers, Daddy rarely came home empty-handed.

Although he kept a few Black Angus cattle on the levee, to "mow" the grass (with the blessing of the Levee Board), Daddy wasn't into animal husbandry. He briefly tried ranching, but after a disease ravaged his herd, dirt farming began to seem more attractive.

## A proud planter

He excelled as a planter, priding himself in geometrically even, weed-free fields, primarily cotton and soybeans. He loved driving visitors along dirt roads between his crops and the weed-infested fields of his neighbors, letting the fields speak for him.

He netted a profit at least fifty years in a row, never speaking of his unusual success until he was elderly.

His passion was growing watermelons. As a boy, he often visited the home of an old sharecropper and was tutored in the art of melon growing. When he began growing his own, Daddy always gave them away.

Over sixty years, his melon give-away total probably reached into the hundreds of thousands.

(He tried to talk me into pumpkin farming, even crawling on his hands and knees alongside me one entire afternoon as we squashed invading beetles in our hands. The venture failed when the truck axle broke while the pumpkins were being hauled to Memphis to be sold for Halloween.)

Daddy usually planted his watermelons on the slopes of his huge, plowed-over Indian mound. When coyotes invaded The Delta, he noticed that they were as fond of melons as the deer, so he tried numerous ways to keep them out, even spending several nights on the mound with a shotgun.

He finally gave up and decided to share.

In his papers, I found his May 13, 1971 "Recipe for growing soybeans." It speaks volumes, advising:

"To work hard, keep the land free of weeds as possible, rotate the crops, wish for good weather, be happy and last but by all means not least, let us not forget our heritage as we were all taught at all times to have faith in God."

## The unfunny perils of brotherhood

Unfortunately, Daddy didn't have a recipe for brotherly love: there was some enmity, which was so subtle I never took notice of it as a child.

Daddy got along famously with six of his siblings, but there was an icy wall between him and his two eldest brothers, George and Alex.

Following Sunday meals at my grandmother's twenty-foot-long dinner table—involving an endless combination of uncles, aunts, and cousins—either Daddy would leave or the two eldest brothers would leave. Like oil and water, they just didn't mix.

I thought nothing of it until my teens. When the pattern got too obvious to ignore, I began asking Daddy about it, without much luck.

Was it because his brothers told him he could fly if he ate chicken wings and left the choicest cuts to them? (A trusting lad, Daddy nearly killed himself when he leapt off the barn, flapping his arms.) That wasn't it.

Maybe it was because Daddy once accidentally discharged his shotgun between his brother George's legs, sinking their boat. Nope.

I thought it was because Alex's wife had snubbed my mother. Close, but no cigar.

Perhaps it was because the family barn burned when Daddy had stored up hay that was too green, causing a fire as it decayed. Nah.

Daddy was plumb mum on his brotherly relations, except to simply say that brother George "wanted me to kiss his ass." Daddy wasn't about to oblige.

I could understand this after an aunt told me that my uncle George advised her to follow his lead and donate most of her money to Mississippi State University. "He told me they would fall all over me and glorify me," she said.

George had made millions, some from when he became king of the hairy vetch market, controlling the world market and setting the legume's seed prices.

George basked in the limelight after donating so much money to MSU that they named a street, a bell tower, and a dining hall (Planet Perry) after him. He felt like the center of that universe.

My response to my aunt was, "Your daddy would roll over in his grave!" She left most of her estate to her family.

When Daddy died at age eighty-eight, I asked one of his younger brothers about the brotherly enmity.

It was their father's fault, he said. "The Cap'n made the mistake of putting George in charge of the younger brothers until George got a farm of his own. Then, he put Alex in charge.

"When we split up the land your daddy got the home place, but Alex kept coming back and 'borrowing' whatever he wanted, without asking permission."

When we went through Daddy's personal files we found a 1938 note from George, in which he briefly asked Daddy to quit calling him Fat, a longtime nickname. If not, he threatened to take steps to avoid Daddy.

Daddy wrote a four-page response, then hand-copied it for his files. (That's what you did before the photocopier came along.)

He lamented the fact that George had not simply spoken to him "man-to-man" on the issue. "I was always under the impression you liked to cut up and have fun," he replied, noting that he had always used nicknames for his friends and had not meant to be derogatory. (Daddy just liked nicknames, and ended up being called Belly, with no complaints, late in life.).

The lengthy apology might have worked better if Daddy had omitted this postscript: "People are as big as the things that annoy them."

### The power of forgiveness

The next letter in the file came from George nearly thirty years later, when Alex became the first sibling to die, at seventy-three. No one had expected Daddy to attend the funeral, but he did. "What a grand thing you did…" said George's letter. "My hat's off to you. I admire you for your fortitude and compassion." He expressed his love and closed with, "Your Brother, George."

Which brings to mind a quote from author Laurence Sterne: "Only the brave know how to forgive…a coward never forgave; it is not in his nature."

The next letter in the file was a letter from my grandmother, thanking Daddy for all he had done for her over the years. The letter states, "My greatest wish is for you all to live in peace and harmony with one another always, even after I have passed to the better life."

I hope all the brothers are enjoying a better life today, finally free of that parasite which infests the living—the ego.

Meanwhile, sibling wrangling still goes on in various family subsets, giving credence to George Santayana's famous line, which says, "Those who cannot remember the past are condemned to repeat it!"

I have refused to take sides, firmly believing that holding a grudge hurts no one but the grudge-holder.

Irish actor Malachy McCourt had this take on it: "Resentment is like taking poison and waiting for the other person to die."


## An ace father

My brother George and I fought all the time. The story of our fight over a gun tells a lot about Daddy's fathering abilities.

While almost any man can sire a child, it's another thing to be a father—to effectively nurture, cherish, nestle, keep tabs on, and stand sentinel over his offspring.

Case in point: at about age nine I was allowed to go into the vast family woods with a .22-caliber rifle, accompanied only by my year-younger brother, George—who promptly spotted a hawk when it was *my* turn to shoot. Back then, every hawk was said to be a chicken hawk and, thus, was fair game.

As some brothers are wont to do, George refused to point out the hawk's whereabouts. So, not to be outdone, I refused to give up my turn. Having been properly trained in gun safety, I calmly propped the rifle against a tree.

He and I were about the same size, so I felt the only way to settle the matter was a boxing match right there in the middle of the old logging road. The brawl began. Suddenly, out of thin air, Daddy materialized and broke it up. It turned out we only *thought* we were alone. He'd been tailing us the whole time.

He's still tailing me! And that's a good thing.

A family coon hunt

Melon Man

High Cotton

"Muscle" Man

The shirt-tail ritual

# THE KING

# CHAPTER 8

## The King

### In control

Daddy believed in self-control and I always thought of him as the king of the farm, in many ways. Maybe that's why he hated to leave; all other territory was foreign to him.

I never saw him cry. When his father died I found Daddy sitting alone very quietly in our living room, but no tears were visible in the unlit room.

Many years later, at my sister's funeral, Daddy asked the family to buck up. "Don't cry," he pleaded. And, although his pleas went unheeded, Daddy kept it all in.

He kept his business affairs to himself, too, preceding any confidential information with, "Between you, me, and the gatepost..."

He kept his own counsel, rarely asking anyone else for advice, except when it came to technical farming support from the county extension agent or the entomologist, whom he called the bug man.

He did mention to me once that he was thinking about retiring, and the only thing I could think to say was, "It would kill you."

It would have killed him, as well, to be dishonest. For example, he once shot and killed a "wild" dog in the yard, only to find it had a collar with a name and address on it. It was James Mitchell's coon dog, Old Red.

Daddy could have simply buried the dog, but Daddy sent Mr. Mitchell a check for $150, imploring him in a letter to "please cash it without telling me you don't deserve it. Then I will be happy and feel good."

He once returned a check to an insurance company when a "stolen" gun was found. The agent was astonished.

## Law and order

Daddy's dexterity with guns may have helped him keep order on the farm. He had a suitcase full of beat-up pistols that he had taken from errant farm workers. One was taken from a burglar captured inside the farm commissary in a stakeout operation.

He once shot a burglar who had been stealing from the store. He obviously wasn't proud of this, as he never mentioned it to his wife and kids. It came out after his funeral, when I asked an uncle about rumors that one of the brothers had killed a man somehow. "It was your Daddy," he said. "The man ran off into the night and nobody knew he'd been shot until days later, when the body began to smell and they found him way off in the weeds."

Daddy did tell about the time he tried to slip up on a poacher in the woods. The man was bent over in the middle of a muddy road, drinking water out of mule hoofprints, with a pistol sticking out of his back pocket. "I thought I could snatch the gun, but it was a stupid mistake," Daddy said. "When he spotted me, he jumped up, whirled around, drew the pistol, and...handed it over to me! He could have shot me if he had wanted to."

I was on a duck-hunting trip with Daddy when he "confiscated" an airplane that we had discovered sitting on a sandbar near the river. Daddy simply let the air out of the plane's tires, left a note, and we went off on our hunt.

When we returned we found two sad-faced Memphians sitting beside the plane. Daddy scoured the sand dunes, found their hidden guns and dead ducks, and drove them to Tunica, where a judge fined them $100 per duck. Daddy then got an air tank, drove them back to the plane, and waved goodbye to them as they lifted off, wiser, poorer, luckless, and duckless.

## Hunting "tails"

Daddy enjoyed taking visitors hunting and this is where his other side, as a joker, showed itself.

He was fond of tossing his guests' hats in the air and shooting them.

On deer hunts, he would cut their shirttails off when they fired at a deer and missed. It's a common hunting tradition to remove a small bit of shirttail, but Daddy snipped with such enthusiasm he'd sometimes cut all the way up to the collar, rendering the shirt worthless.

This backfired on him once, when he was ripping into the expensive wool Pendleton shirt worn by his son-in-law, Barney Eaton. Barney bided his time until it was too late. He then confessed, "Mr. Jack, I borrowed your shirt."

Another hunting expedition nearly backfired on Daddy. When I brought a fraternity brother from Connecticut home to visit with me, Daddy suggested a snipe hunt, a fake hunt where you leave the victim stranded and "holding the bag."

When my friend guffawed knowingly, Daddy broke out a bird book and showed him a picture of a snipe. Soon Daddy had this guy decked out in camouflage, with a headlight strapped to his forehead. We couldn't find a bag, so we had to resort to an aluminum-framed laundry hamper on wheels.

However, my friend was pretty smart and rode all the way back home on the rear bumper of the Jeep, after Daddy had left me behind to watch the ditch where we had deposited the "hunter."

When Daddy got home he found the victim standing behind the Jeep and, believe it or not, actually talked him into going back into the ditch, where he was left holding the bag a second time!

### Family coon hunts

Daddy loved to take family and friends on nighttime coon-hunting romps through the woods, leading his followers to think they were hopelessly lost in the darkness—until they happened upon a campfire setup, complete with hot dogs, marshmallows, and cold drinks.

Going into the woods, he would alert newcomers to be on the lookout for the bobcat tree, a sycamore with a dead bobcat hanging from an overhanging limb. When that got old, he took down the dried-out cat carcass, leaving little Duke's stuffed panda hanging in its place.

Leaving the woods, there inevitably would be a Jeep race home.

Daddy would usually pull ahead by plowing through mud holes while others took the drier detour routes.

Once, the only Jeep that Daddy had to beat was Uncle Clyde's. As Clyde roared up the road that angled up the levee, Daddy simply zoomed straight up the embankment, almost going airborne as he powered his Jeep over the top of the levee on the way to victory.

Daddy loved competition. And he liked to win.

In his seventies, he dared one of the fiftyish farm hands to a race, with a co-conspirator designated to hold the younger man back by grabbing his belt. When the younger man bolted free, Daddy couldn't resist the urge to give it his best shot, tumbling head over heels when he pulled a muscle.

## Family fireworks

At family picnics there were all kinds of races, with men's, women's, and various children's categories. The women's race was usually the most hilarious, considering that one aunt was overweight and the runners would hold their dresses above their knees.

On July Fourth and at Christmas, Daddy would buy a truckload of fireworks, including buzz-bombs, firecrackers, roman candles, sparklers, and mortars. Sometimes he would get everyone on top of the levee and give each person a bunch of foot-tall mortars, asking everyone to light them all at once and run like hell.

The sky would light up as the explosions crackled overhead. A few minutes later we'd hear a competing salvo from Uncle Bobby Cox's farm about a mile away.

## Farm teams

Daddy also organized competitions among the farm hands, including watermelon-eating contests, which were usually won by one worker who'd suck down seeds and all.

In a corner of the store was a big, wooden barrel full of baseball gear, made available to our farm team, so they could train and compete with rival teams from nearby farms.

These players were really talented, though not fully up-to-date on the nuances of the game. Bill Selman, a cousin from California, begged them to let him join their practice and left them writhing on the ground, howling with laughter, when this little white boy laid down the first bunt they'd ever seen.

Sometimes Daddy would toss the football with George and me, usually bailing out after a few minutes to get back to work. So George and I resolved to teach some of the farm kids how to play.

The game was totally alien to them and we gave up after one of them, nicknamed Buck Naked, grabbed the ball, jumped the ditch at the edge of the yard, and took off running across an adjoining cotton field. It took us a while to get the ball back.

## Muscle man

When Daddy played pitch with us he'd have to throw the ball underhanded because it hurt his throwing arm. His left arm was even less flexible because he had somehow split the bicep on that arm, leaving him with a huge, permanently bulging muscle, which he loved to show off in public, pretending to be flexing it. He kept the other, normal, arm out of sight, so no one would be tempted to make comparisons.

He prided himself in finding the season's first cotton bloom in the county nearly every year and would take it to the *Tunica Times* for his prize, a free subscription to the newspaper. He would pose for a photo, holding up the bloom with the bulging bicep on display. It was just one of his many jokes.

# Never a Dull Moment

*Old college drinking buddy, George Hayley, provided a constant stream of foolishness*

Below: the store and office-wall mementoes

Deer butt

Fake "deer trophy"

"Two Bald Headed Dudes"

# CHAPTER 9

## The Joker

### The fun closet

You might say Daddy was a closet comedian, because he had a closet full of gags to prove it. He called it the fun closet and kept it under lock and key—until we had a visitor, which was a rare occasion.

One Christmas I tried to get Daddy a present from the Fun Shop, a small Memphis store that specialized in gags and magic tricks. Each time the store owner made a suggestion, I'd reply, "He's already got that."

This went on for a while, until the exasperated owner demanded, "Who's this gift for?"

"Jack Perry," I replied.

"I'm sorry," he said, dejectedly, "he's already got everything we have!"

One year our maid, Chris, came up with one of the best Christmas gifts Daddy ever got. She gave him a mechanical Frankenstein doll, which would growl and wave its arms fiercely until its pants fell down, revealing striped boxer shorts. Then, the growling would stop and the monster's face would glow red with embarrassment.

From that day on, every time friends and relatives visited, out came the Frankenstein monster. Before starting the motor, Daddy would challenge some male in the group to "Mock the Monster," adding, "If you do everything he does I'll give you five dollars."

It's amazing how many guys will drop their trousers for five bucks!

Although Daddy's fun closet was already packed with gags and magic tricks, Frankenstein was truly the gift that kept on giving.

## Let the show begin

Here's how it went when a first-time visitor showed up. First, Daddy would name you. Rather than try to remember your name, he'd stick you with a nickname that he could remember. For example, his four grandsons were Moose (Pace), Columbus (Christopher), Possum (Jack), and Coon (Rob).

Then he might start up a conversation that sounded like a vaudeville routine, in which he exaggerated his deafness, such as this exchange with a fourteen-year-old boy:

"How old are you boy?"

"Fourteen."

"Fart-teen?"

"No, sir." (Blush.)

"Do you dip [snuff]?"

"No, sir."

"Women?"

"Sometimes." (Blush.)

"Summer time?"

Then the magic would happen.

## Magic man

First, Daddy would make a nickel disappear—if he had on a shirt with long sleeves. He had mastered the art of snapping his fingers and propelling a nickel up the sleeve of his outstretched arm.

When he'd lower his arm the nickel would slide back into his hand and then reappear, usually after being "pulled" from someone's ear.

As he got older the nickel started disappearing across the room behind him, missing his sleeve. I drew a cartoon of him once, showing a pile of nickels at his feet and a caption that had him saying, "*Now...* watch *THIS* nickel disappear."

After the nickel trick, Daddy would then start trekking back and forth to the fun closet in his bedroom, bringing out gag after gag— ranging from a fake book (which would nearly electrocute you when you opened it) to magic tricks. The fun would sometimes go on for an hour or so.

## The disappearing woman

Daddy's magic was no match for the famous disappearing act performed one day by Aunt Ewee. I was strolling with her behind Miss Sallie's house when she suddenly vanished into thin air.

I was about six and was on the brink of getting scared when I looked down and saw her clinging to the lip of a concrete septic tank in the ground. She had stepped on the concrete lid covering the hole and it gave way somehow, plunging her into a place none of us wants to go.

Her son, Jack Selman, was with us and he joined me in holding her up by her arms while we yelled for help. Some adults arrived shortly and pulled her to safety.

As they carried Ewee into Grandmomma's house, I lingered for a while and looked for turtles in the broth below. All I could see were tur...

## Deflating egos

Most of Daddy's tricks did not involve magic, but revolved around gag toys. On the rare occasions we got Daddy to go to dinner in Memphis, he would bring some of the gags with him.

One memorable event was a family dinner at the exclusive Rivermont Club overlooking the Mississippi River. The entertainment was provided by a musical trio, led by a pompous little piano player sporting a pencil-thin moustache.

I was a newspaper reporter then and Daddy borrowed my press card, pulled out a camera, and persuaded the maestro to pose in a ridiculously foppish position in front of the piano for a news shot.

The victim's fake grin evolved into a slow-burn grimace that would have been worthy of a Three Stooges movie, as a spring-loaded mouse jumped out of the camera, flew across the stage, and thumped harmlessly against his puffed-out chest.

## Elia Kazan was no exception

One day, when I was about ten, I came home from school and found famed movie director Elia Kazan eating saltines and hoop cheese at our kitchen table with Daddy.

He had come from Hollywood, California, to our farmhouse near Hollywood, Mississippi, Daddy explained, to scout locations for an upcoming movie titled *Baby Doll.*

Since my parents had been married by an old Episcopalian minister who was Tennessee Williams' grandfather, Kazan had been directed to my father by the famous playwright soon after they had completed filming *A Streetcar Named Desire.*

This long-faced immigrant from Turkey was an ex-Communist who had become a lightning rod when he chose to name names before the McCarthy inquisition and had been allowed to continue making movies in Hollywood while members of his former Communist cell were being blacklisted.

To Daddy, he was just more fodder for practical jokes, and he was firing them at Kazan faster than Joe McCarthy could say, "Are you now or have you ever been a member of the Communist Party?" After pummeling Kazan with a passel of pranks, Daddy ended up taking him on his patented tour of the farm.

## The suicide run

The tour ended with the suicide run. It started with an innocent pickup-truck tour of the farm, with Daddy driving up and down the dusty turn-rows, explaining the intricacies of cotton, wheat, soybeans, watermelons, and cattle—rambling on and on, ad nauseam.

The tour always ended on the levee, which had a gravel road on top. As always, Daddy would be waxing eloquent about the endless, flat fields on one side of the levee when his pickup would "accidentally" plunge off the far side and career down the steep slope of grass toward the woods.

Of course, he'd always just barely bring the truck under control at the last second, before it could plow into the trees. The trick was to make sure the panic-stricken passenger didn't bail out. (One did once, but he wasn't injured). Then, Daddy would break out laughing, with most of the victims joining in after realizing they'd just had a free roller-coaster ride.

## A jackass response

Kazan, I'm told, appeared not to see the humor in the situation. He later sent Daddy copies of photos he'd taken on the farm—and underneath a picture of a mule I noticed Kazan had penned in "Jack Perry."

Daddy had already rejected Kazan's offer to film scenes on the farm. Daddy was "The King of the Farm," and he didn't want any city slickers in his cotton patches!

To paraphrase the bandit chief in *The Treasure of the Sierra Madre:* "Film crews!?! We don' need no stinkin' film crews!!!"

At last, Kazan had been blacklisted in Hollywood—or at least on a farm near Hollywood, Mississippi.

In the late '70s I met Kazan again at an international booksellers convention in Atlanta. He was holed up in a back room, flailing away at an old manual typewriter, presumably writing one of his novels.

I introduced myself and asked him if he remembered his wild ride down the levee.

He said that he did, and turned back to his typing without so much as offering cheese and crackers. I'm naming names.

## An equal-opportunity gagster

While many of Daddy's victims were most deserving, Daddy was an equal-opportunity gagster.

My earliest memory of being victimized was when I left a fishing pole stuck into the bank of a rivulet to walk over the levee for lunch. After eating, I ran back over the levee to find I had caught a rubber hotdog.

When my sister, Jett, had a preteen Halloween party, Daddy

persuaded his old friend George "Country Fool" Hayley to dress up as a witch, complete with glowing lightbulb eyes and pointed hat, and ride up on a borrowed white horse, whose blind eyes were covered by an eerie, milk-white film.

Little brother Duke was convinced it was "a weal, weal witch."

## Playing 'possum

When Daddy came into possession of a batch of live baby 'possums he started mailing them, one a day, to a friend, Neil Block of Tunica. Neil says the postmaster complained and Daddy mailed the remaining batch all together in one parting shot. They all arrived alive and unsquashed, I'm told.

Daddy's old college buddy, George "Country Fool" (aka CF) Hayley, was the brunt of most jokes. Daddy took up golf for awhile with CF and couldn't resist exchanging CF's putting ball with a ball that wobbled, or letting CF tee up with a trick ball that exploded and went streaking down the fairway, leaving a pluming trail of smoke. This was after Daddy urged him to "knock the fire out of it!"

Daddy once propped a mounted deer head between two trees in the woods and convinced CF to keep shooting when the deer refused to go down. Duke inherited the bullet-riddled trophy and has it on his wall today.

Some of Daddy's humor was off-color. As a self-employed farmer, he was beholden to few men, and as a consequence he was not very constrained by most social conventions. He thought nothing of thrusting out his little finger to a total stranger. "Pull," he would command, releasing a single staccato fart just as the digit was yanked. His timing was always perfect.

He would then make a pitiful face, laced with considerable charisma and charm. Soon, he and the startled stranger (male or female) would be laughing together, bonding, social barriers down: fellow pilgrims on the journey of life. He always seemed to get away with it.

Momma would just roll her eyes. It was useless to do anything else.

## Life plays its own joke

Daddy was blessed with good health most of his life, and never had a headache after he quit drinking in his thirties.

When something would fail he would make the best of it. For example, while recovering from eye surgery for a torn retina, he would answer the door with dark glasses, a cane, and a cup, begging for money.

He said that in the hospital an old fellow kept coming into his room to chat, finally asking: "Mr. Perry, may I ask what your ailment is?"

"I told him I had a torn retina and he said, 'Mr. Perry, them hemorrhoids can be bad!'"

Except for such minor problems, Daddy made it to eighty in such good mental and physical health that he often said he thought he easily could make it to one hundred.

One spring day, in his mideighties, he awoke before dawn and headed into the woods, alone, to hunt for wild turkeys.

After the hunt he had to walk home several miles because his truck battery had gone dead. He retrieved his truck and headed to his watermelon patch on the Indian mound, working there until dark.

The next day one knee began to ache. Over time his legs went, first one, then the other. He began falling down, sometimes lying on the floor for hours, trying to get up and too proud to call for help.

He couldn't get out of the bathtub one day and lay in the cold water for hours before Duke took the hinges off the locked door and rescued him.


## A driving force

Even so, Daddy continued to drive long after he should have been stopped. Driving across Highway 61, he pulled out directly in front of an oncoming car. Luckily, no one was seriously hurt in the ensuing wreck and the injured family accepted Daddy's offer of monetary restitution without threatening a lawsuit.

That's when we found out that Daddy had not renewed his driver's license for years. When the state trooper asked for his license, Daddy simply replied, "Can't you see I'm old enough to drive?!?"

When my brothers finally took his car keys away, he began borrowing the old car he had given to the maid.

One day he was spotted driving the car at a high rate of speed down the cotton turnrows. When my brother George caught up to him and asked what he was doing, Daddy explained that the car engine was overheating and he was simply trying to cool it off.

That's when we realized his mind was going.

## Even the FBI couldn't help

For some reason Daddy became obsessed with the notion that someone was circulating a photograph of him around the country. To placate him, my brothers assigned a grandson to drive Daddy to the FBI offices in Jackson, Mississippi, to settle the matter once and for all.

Forewarned, an FBI agent took "notes" and launched an "investigation," sending Daddy home fully satisfied.

Daddy developed congestive heart failure and eventually was hospitalized with kidney failure, gradually drowning in his own fluids. Doctors assured us it was a painless way to go.

He gave up control peacefully. His going was like the loss of an old-growth tree in the forest—it left a big hole in the canopy of our lives.

*A newspaper shot with Daddy showing off "the first cotton bloom" of the year and his huge "muscle".*

*With his kids*

*"Throwing" his voice*

*Daddy & Duke at work in store office*

*With grandsons "Columbus" (Christopher) & "Possum" (Jack II)*

*Jett's "Playhouse"*

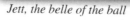

*Jett, the belle of the ball*

# CHAPTER 10

## Big Deals

### The Ghost of Christmas Past

Every Christmas morning I wake up and expect a call from the Ghost of Christmas Past.

Invariably, the phone rings and one of my sons tries to beat me to it: "Christmas Gift!" It's the game Daddy always played with the farm hands. They had to say it so fast it came out "Crimmagiff," because whoever said it first was supposed to receive a gift from the loser.

Daddy didn't lose much, but when he lost, he'd try to turn the tables, sticking his hand out, palm up, and demanding, "Hand it here!" Then he'd laugh and proceed to give a gift.

When he *won,* he also gave a gift!

Now he's a ghost and every Christmas I think back to the way he and one farm worker, Willie Duckett, played the game in earnest, even when they were in their eighties.

"Duck" was overweight and waddled a bit, looking a bit like Jazz-legend Louis "Satchmo" Armstrong on steroids.

At first light each Christmas we could always find Daddy creeping around the house, peeking out every window until finally he could locate Duck—who'd be creeping around the yard, hoping to win the game once in his life. Because Daddy had home-field advantage, Duck was doomed.

And what a wonderful doom it was. Duck would always get some goodies and a big glass of whisky.

Duck was the last of legions of farm workers who used to show up to play the game when Daddy was much younger. It was like a horde of Inspector Clouseaus trying to surprise the wily Cato.

One year Daddy perched himself at an attic window, yelled "Christmas Gift!" and baptized the whole lot with water. Another time he substituted the traditional glasses of whisky with small shots of vinegar, encouraging his victims to down it in one gulp. Laughter was always the order of the day.

After a morning of frivolity at the house we would drive a truckload of gifts around the farm, playing Santa Claus with each farm family.

We gave out goodies that were a far cry from the Christmas gifts Daddy got as a child (usually just some nuts and fruit). In good years he and his eight siblings got an orange apiece.

## Christmas in July

The Christmas spirit also visited the farm each summer, when Daddy would grow about five acres of watermelons to give away. Whenever we went to Memphis he'd haul a load for waitresses and salespeople he knew.

He'd fill our yard with melons and "friends" would drive up and ask for a free watermelon, sometimes leaving with their cars nearly dragging the ground.

Daddy had one rule: If you got a green melon, you could exchange it for a ripe one—provided you returned the green one. When one farm worker came back, claiming the first was green, Daddy asked, "Where is the green one?"

The worker's reply: "I et it." Daddy laughed and gave him another. As the years wore on, many melon recipients simply got too old and feeble to make the trip to the farm. Daddy simply hired a crew to drive around and make deliveries. To him, it was Christmas all summer. As Elvis sang, "Why can't every day be like Christmas?" Why not? "Christmas Gift!"

## The playhouse and Elvis Presley

There's another Elvis song that brings back memories. It's one where he asks his girlfriend if she wants to "play house" with him.

Daddy loved his only daughter, Jett, with a passion, so when she asked for a small playhouse, like the miniature houses you find in backyards all across the South, Daddy was eager to please.

Using farm carpenters, he built her an 850-square-foot, knotty-pine-paneled, one-room beauty, complete with an adjoining half-bath. It cost $5,000, which was a big sum back then.

Later, on a trip to Jett's dance studio in Memphis, Momma had Jett, George, and me in tow when she agreed to give one of the Memphis students a ride home.

That was a mistake, because the student's family had a television set. When we stopped by to leave off the student and saw the family's television set with a snowy picture of some guy called Hopalong Cassidy, Jett wanted a TV. So, as soon as Tunica County could receive a decent signal, a television set went into her playhouse.

## The invasion of television

That's when the playhouse ceased to be Jett's sole domain and evolved into a place for the whole family to watch programs like *The Original Amateur Hour* with host Ted Mack.

We were bombarded with advertising such as the dancing human cigarette packages, featuring a big adult female package and a little girl package. It made smoking look cool and soon we kids were borrowing cigarettes on the sly from our cook. We had been corrupted.

However, this was much better than the "rabbit tobacco" George and I had smoked earlier. Because we thought it involved rabbit hair instead of a weed, it turned out to be a hare-brained idea, leaving us coughing and unable to speak for a little while. We had *hare-yngitis*, I think.

When Daddy joined the TV viewing audience we watched whatever he wanted to see, such as "prize fighting," complete with scantily clad beauties who marched around the boxing ring during breaks, sporting signs that announced the number of the upcoming round. I liked that part.

The Gillette advertising would tell us, "To look sharp, and be on the ball; to feel sharp and be on the ball" we should use their products for the best, closest shave of all. I figured that in about twelve years or so I'd try their products.

When he got the TV to himself, our little brother, Duke, would watch some character named Winky Dink and draw all over the screen with a crayon—until Daddy gave in and bought him the magic film that was supposed to be adhered to the screen for drawing.

## Beating the heat

There's no good way to adequately describe the oppressive summer heat of The Delta. With its high humidity, it's like an ocean of heat, layered, brutally pressing down with its own weight, causing shimmering mirages and sending "dust devils" spinning across the fields, like they're trying to escape to some cooler place.

The heat carried over into the night, forcing us to sleep on sweat-soaked sheets, with an electric attic fan and floor fans futilely striving to provide us with relief.

Some people measure time as B.C. and A.D. Another way to divide it up is B.A.C. and A.A.C.—before and after air-conditioning.

When we got air-conditioning life changed overnight. After we reached the A.A.C. epoch we'd sit in the air-conditioned playhouse and watch whatever was on TV, when we should have been playing outside. It really didn't matter what was on our three measly, snowy channels. It was *cool!*

## Goodbye to parlor games

I think we really lost something when parlor games disappeared. These may be tomorrow's "good old days" for someone; not for me. I had mine in the '40s, pre-TV, when ordinary Americans actually entertained each other. And, although we'd occasionally huddle around the radio and "watch" radio programs in our minds (using imagination to envision the characters), kids mostly spent nonworking hours playing with each other.

Some evenings Daddy would regale us with made-up Jimmy Turtle tales, or we'd perform family talent shows. At family picnics, everyone—men, women, and children— joined in all kinds of races:

dashes, sack races, and three-legged debacles in which racing pairs each strapped two legs together and tried to run.

At big indoor family get-togethers adults and children would play parlor games. In one, a designated "counter" would go from person to person on each syllable of this chant: "Wire, briar, limberlock, three geese in a flock, one flew east, one flew west, one flew over the cuckoo's nest!

"O...U...T spells *out*, you dirty dishrag, *you*!"

If you were last, it meant you had to leave the room and return on someone's back. The way you answered certain questions determined whether you got bucked off gently or slammed onto an imaginary feather bed. Whatever you asked for, you got the opposite.

One game required an unsuspecting victim to stand blindfolded on a folded, floor-level ironing board. He was made to believe it was being lifted toward the ceiling, when he was actually being lifted only a couple of inches as everyone else got closer to the floor, shouting encouragement.

After bumping his head on the "ceiling" (a book held over his head), the victim would feel his platform wobble until he fell off, convinced he was plunging to his death.

Another game, Pinch-and-no-laugh, involved everyone standing in a circle. The object was for everyone, one at a time, to pinch the face of the person to the right and not laugh. The victim of this game ended up with soot or lipstick all over his face, laughing innocently with the rest of the players.

### Is youth wasted on the young?

In the 1970s I decided to stop in Mountville, Georgia, "Oldest Settlement in Troup County," to find its oldest resident, the late Buena Owens, eighty-eight, and reminisce about even older good old days.

She remembered kids playing with everything from corncobs to pottery shards. "Back then it was all you could do to make a living," she said. "Maybe kids would get one toy for Christmas and some fruit. Now, kids don't seem to know nothin' to play. All they want is to watch television or get in a car and ride, ride, ride. They don't know how to walk nowhere.

"People want their kids to have everything 'cause they didn't have it themselves when they were kids. Ain't nothin' left for some kids to get. I believe people were happier then."


## Who let the lions out?

The worst thing about owning a TV was that Daddy no longer took us to rodeos, ice shows, professional wrestling, or circuses.

I guess that was all right, though, since he soon figured out that professional wrestling was fake.

And, the last time he took us to the Shrine Circus, several lions escaped from their center-ring cage and ran up the aisle right past us, on the way out the door. We stayed inside while the lions roamed around the streets of Memphis, where they were soon recaptured.

I never will forget the terror on the face of the circus sales boy, who threw about twenty open bags of popcorn into the air in a successful effort to divert the lions as they ran past him.

Daddy followed up the TV with a pool table, further proof that the playhouse was no longer Jett's domain.

However, Jett seized control again when she reached her teens. She would hole up inside, making out with boyfriends such as fullback football star Charles Smith, nicknamed Suitcase because he could carry the load.

Jett and her peers introduced me to rhythm-and-blues songs with lyrics along these lines: "I'm like a one-eyed cat, peeping in a seafood store…" (To aggravate her, I changed the lyrics to "seeping in a pee-food store.")

Then, we made a fateful trip to Memphis that led to regular dance parties in the playhouse, where Tunica-area teens often bopped the night away.


## Was it Elvis Presley or Albert Preston?

The first thing I remember about the trip was Robert Earl Lane's stallion staked out in a grassy patch in front of the Pure gasoline station at Robinsonville, along Highway 61. The horse was performing phallic gymnastics.

When you're a horny horse, without the benefit of a mare, the best you can do is to slap your belly; it certainly beats plowing through dirt, which is what he could have done. (I thought I was imagining things, but I later saw a zebra doing the same thing in some nature film.)

It took all the willpower I could muster not to shout, "Look at *that*!!!" I restrained myself because Daddy was driving my sister and two of her girlfriends to see some singer in Memphis, and the last thing they needed on this trip was to see a pony in a state of arousal. They were already agitated enough.

I got to go along and bring a buddy, Sterling "Sterl" Owen, so Daddy wouldn't be outnumbered by females. Sterl and I didn't quite get it, but we were only about fourteen. The girls were two years older and *so* much more mature.

"Are you girls ready to see Albert Preston?" Daddy continually teased them. For a while they giggled and protested, saying "That's not his name!!!" After awhile they gave up. Albert Preston it would be.

We arrived at Russwood Park, a baseball field used by the Memphis Chicks, a minor-league team. We settled into our field-level seats along the third-base line just before the crowd erupted.

"Albert Preston" mounted a semi-truck bed near home plate and launched into a set of songs, punctuated by his patented pelvic moves.


### Girls gone wild

The girls went wild, screaming, "Elvis! Elvis!"

Sterl and I sat quietly, marveling at the sea of hysteria surrounding us. We didn't quite know what to think.

We had no idea we were getting in on the ground floor of a singing career that later would be regarded as one of the most important phenomena in American entertainment history.

There was this young man, possibly nineteen or twenty, who had this golden voice that at once was bass, baritone, and tenor. He had been born down the road in Tupelo, Mississippi, on January 1, 1935, to parents so poor that they had to bury his deceased twin brother, Jesse Garon, in a shoebox.

I didn't quite get it, but the girls got it. When Elvis finished his hip-swiveling show, he strode across the grass toward us, and disappeared into the dugout below. My sister and her friends made a frenzied foray onto the field and began pulling up the grass he had stepped on. They were extremely proud of their souvenirs.

On the way out of Memphis we stopped at Kay's barbecue, which offered some of the best eating a barbecue aficionado could want. We went inside and the girls began cooling off.

There was a debate over what the sign on the table meant by "pizza pie." What kind of dessert, we all wanted to know, was "pissa" pie?

Then Daddy started the girls giggling again, "Well, girls, how'd you like Albert Preston?"

Sitting at the next table were two hoods wearing black leather jackets and sporting slicked-back, ducktail hairdos. They were looking at each other with disbelief. Finally one sneered to the other, "He don't even know his *name*!!!"


## Getting hip

The hoods got it. The girls got it. Daddy would eventually get it, learning to say Elvis Presley and taking Momma to sold-out Elvis concerts years later, after it became respectable.

Sterl and I were a little slow on the uptake, but in the following months we began to get it. Spending considerably more than the $10.75 that Elvis' parents spent on his first guitar, we got ourselves some "strings" and began to learn as many licks as we could.

Sterl got so good at the guitar that he could have made a career of it. He formed a popular folk-sing trio at Vanderbilt University and later created a country music group called the Turnrow Cowboys. He even became a co-owner of a restaurant called The Hollywood, so the Cowboys would have a place to perform.

On Friday nights Sterl featured a black piano player named Muriel, who would later achieve some fame.

Originally in the town of Hollywood, the restaurant was moved to an old commissary building in Robinsonville, where it is still open today, under new owners. It's famous for two things: french-fried dill pickles and being featured, during Sterl's co-ownership, by Marc Cohn in his famous song of the year, *Walking in Memphis*.

"Now Muriel plays piano every Friday at the Hollywood," the song says. In it, Marc "plays a little number" at Muriel's request, and Muriel asks Marc, who's Jewish, "Are you a Christian, child?" Marc's reply: "Ma'am, I am tonight!"

If you view the song's video you can see Sterl slow-dancing with a partner at The Hollywood, just like he used to do at the playhouse dances.

Sterl is certainly a Christian and has performed almost every Sunday night for seven years at "The Oasis" worship service at the Tunica Methodist Church.

I, on the other hand, rarely pick up my guitar these days. When I was twenty-one, I traveled alone around the world, taking my first guitar with me. I later added a used Flamenco guitar in Spain and left my first guitar, a Gibson, in Turkey.

## Mangled Elvis

I learned probably more than one hundred folk songs and sang for my supper all around the globe, acquiring a few groupies along the way, including a beautiful Thai girlfriend who got me a one-night job in a Bangkok nightclub. Performing mostly before American GIs, I launched into some Kingston Trio songs, but soon the GIs began yelling, "Play some Elvis." That was the end of my professional singing career.

Some Thai guy got up on the stage and gyrated like Elvis, mangling the lyrics, such as "You ah nubbuh buh buh how-dough" instead of "You ain't nothin' but a hound dog." The crowd went wild. Even bad Elvis music is better than having no Elvis music at all, I learned.

## Catastrophe strikes

Two catastrophes finished off my musical aspirations, years later.

I bought a Flamenco guitar in Spain and sometimes I would play it in bed before going to sleep, setting it on the floor when I got sleepy. One morning I got up and stepped *in* it! I tried gluing it back together, but gave up after realizing it was nothing more than a glue-tar. After grieving for the appropriate amount of time, I replaced it with a cheap Yamaha model.

The next catastrophe saw me lose my so-so singing voice to thyroid-cancer surgery. That was more than twenty years ago, and I'm just grateful that I've lived long enough to see my two sons happily married and to become a grandfather.

## Massive radiation

Doctors theorized that the cancer was caused by massive doses of radiation, which I had received as a teenager. Because Jett, George, and I all had mild acne, Momma took us to an idiot dermatologist in Memphis who treated us many, many times by exposing us to X-rays for extremely long periods, minutes at a time.

Back then the danger of X-rays wasn't widely known. We used to go in Buster Brown shoe stores and play with an X-ray machine that customers could use to see how well shoes fit.

George, who had the least exposure, has had bouts with many non-cancerous tumors.

Jett, who had the most treatments, died of brain cancer on October 4, 1968, a few days after turning twenty-nine. It was devastating to the family. She left two young daughters. I'm proud to say that they grew up to be fine young ladies—with a lot of help from Momma—and now have big families of their own.

## Elvis leaves the building

Less than a decade after Jett's death, Elvis died on August 18, 1977, as heralded in the Memphis newspaper saved for me by Momma (along with papers heralding "less important" things like wars and assassinations). He was forty-two.

When I bought my first house in Memphis, the Realtor drove me past Elvis' first house in Memphis. It was a modest ranch-style home at 1034 Audubon Drive, where Elvis lived for a year before swapping it for Graceland, a fourteen-acre estate where he would have more privacy.

The Audubon house was for sale. It might have been a great investment, but I didn't even want to go in and look at it. That's because I didn't get it.

Elvis is worshipped today as "The King," and some followers have even formed a "Presleyterian" church, but I still don't really get it. Don't they know that he was simply Albert Preston?

Both Elvis and Jett are survived by the playhouse.

When my grandparents died, Daddy inherited their home place and his homesite was transferred to Aunt Ewee. She had our old house removed, giving it away, but kept the playhouse, adding a kitchenette so she could stay there during her many visits from California.

Now that Ewee has died, the little house is owned by her sons.

I hope they'll let it stand, as a testament to another day and a pretty girl whose life was much too short.


## Opening the fun closet

When Daddy died, we unlocked the fun closet, only to find that nearly all of his gags were gone, presumably given away as he started to wind down.

More important were the treasures he had locked away—letters which pertained to important matters.

Never owning a copy machine, Daddy had meticulously hand-copied his own letters for his records.

Many of the letters were sad, particularly the incoming letter from his son-in-law that detailed the initial diagnosis of my sister Jett's eventually fatal brain cancer.

I was reminded of the time when Daddy and I went to Memphis to see a stage show by the Great Blackstone, a famous magician. I think

I was about six.

We were seated near the front row and the next thing I knew Daddy was invited onto the stage when Blackstone asked for volunteers. Blackstone took Daddy's watch without Daddy having any idea it was gone.

That was the first time I had seen Daddy dumbstruck. The next time was when God took Jett.

When I read the letters I could feel the fun being sucked out of the closet.

Duck, with Daddy

Miss Sallie's cook,
Miss Willie Pope

Chris, our beloved maid, with second
husband, Rock Sims

Hog Killing

Baptizing

"Crookleg"
Jack Johnson

Rock, Coot, Chris & Jack Whitley Perry II

# CHAPTER 11

## The Hands

### A time warp in India

In 2007 I agreed to lead a Rotary International Group Study Exchange team to the agricultural state of Andhra Pradesh, India. One day I was in a small farming village just as workers were filtering in from fields where they'd toiled for the equivalent of pennies a day.

Still full of energy, they clustered together, conversing and drinking chai, Indian tea. They seemed content. Though they owned little, they had something priceless: each other, a sense of community.

Suddenly I was overcome by nostalgia, plunging into a time warp when I was a child on a 1940s Mississippi Delta farm, now as alien to me as that far-off village in India.

On our farm each family of workers had its own cypress-sided, tin-roofed home, nestled in its own tree-studded oasis in the middle of flat Delta cropland. Each of these oases had a garden, a mule pen, a hog pen, chickens, a water pump, an outhouse, and a woodpile that rose in the summer and ebbed in the winter.

The predawn pealing of the plantation bell roused workers and was followed by another bell at first light, signaling the beginning of the work day. Other bells flanked lunchtime and then punctuated the day at quitting time, usually at dusk. Each family worked the land around their house.

It has been estimated that the workers probably worked about 150 days a year, on average, basically taking winter and rainy days off. That is not to say that there weren't a lot of chores to be done during the "off" days, such as hauling firewood and tending to gardens. It took a lot of effort in those days just to stay alive.

On the days they worked in the fields it was intense, from first light to full dark, or from "can to can't," as they said, referring to the duration of visibility. May to July involved planting, plowing and hoeing in an all-out war on weeds and grass. Late August to November was the time to focus on picking the cotton, in a race to harvest the crop before rain could stain the fiber and reduce its value.

Daddy probably worked about 300 days a year, rising before dawn and often quitting well after dark. There was always something to tend to. He'd often drag into the house, eat supper, and get one of his kids to massage his aching legs before going to sleep.

In the back of his mind there was always a little worry going on, all 365 days a year—but not usually as much as in 1930, when he went from May 10 to September 15 without a rain. That was the year the mules and cows got turned loose in the woods to fend for themselves (the woods caught fire and Daddy said he could remember the awful smell of burning mules).

He also remembered the year his father was holding out for a dollar a pound for his cotton, eventually settling for five cents per pound, when the bottom fell out of the market.

Daddy's worry would turn to stoicism when the worst thing possible finally happened. He'd simply shrug it off, saying, "That's all in it; that's part of it."

Daddy thought my brother and I had needed to worry some, too, and assigned us our own cotton crop when we were about seven and eight. We plowed with mules, chopped with hoes, and then dragged a huge cotton sack at picking time.

And, although we did most all the work, we only got two-thirds of the profit, since Daddy made Jett the so-called bookkeeper, giving her a third even though she did no work at all. Looking back on the unfairness of it, I think we should have formed a children's labor union. We could have called it the E.I.E.I.O.

## Symbiosis of sorts

In nature, there are conditions where two dissimilar organisms unite in an intimate association for the mutual benefit of both. It's called *symbiosis*. I once heard a corporate motivational speaker define it simply as "one plus one equals three."

After Reconstruction ("The Second Civil War") the whites and blacks had to strike a new deal. The whites had the land, the capital, and farm-management skills. Most of the blacks were not educated well enough to run their own businesses and, further, lacked opportunities. Nearly all returned to farm labor, eager to work for themselves, albeit on someone else's land.

The compromise throughout most of the South was some variation or permutation of the sharecropping system, where the workers were provided a house and lot for gardens and animal pens. The landowner paid the taxes and provided a doctor when needed. Seed, fertilizer, mules, and equipment were provided by the landowner, and living expenses were doled out throughout the year in a system called furnish.

The landowners generally sold the crop, then split the profits (at varying percentages, usually halves) after deductions for charges at the company store.

On some farms with unscrupulous owners, the workers got nothing at year end or even owed money. A friend of mine in Georgia recounted the story of how his father paid a new farm worker his profits at the end of the year. The worker broke into tears, exclaiming, "You the first white man ever let me make any money!"

From all accounts, Daddy and Granddaddy always ran their farms in an open and honest way, paying their workers all that was due them, and sometimes more. Some of the workers were frugal and saved; others got rid of their earnings as fast as they could.

Gradually, sharecropping gave way to various systems of hourly wages, with the homes still furnished for free.

No matter how you cut it, the planter-worker arrangement of my youth had Faustian elements. I'm not here to defend the system. It was what it was.

To many outsiders, the whole situation was wretched. It was far from perfect—but, viewed through the lens of childhood innocence, there was much good in it.


## Pay day

My favorite time was Saturday, when most of the farm's families would congregate at the farm store, or commissary, with an easygoing familiarity. To them, talking was an art—and I was an eager listener.

Daddy would be in his back office, "paying off," as a line of laughing workers snaked down the middle of the store. Daddy would yell, "Next'un!" as each worker exited with his pay.

My childhood job was to sell a variety of goods, including Moon Pies, big cinnamon cookies called Stage Planks, candies, canned goods such as salmon and Vienna (Vy-eenie) sausages, pickled pigs feet, pickled eggs, salted pork, clothes, flour, nails, coal oil (kerosene), and drinks, ranging from RC Colas (Arra Cees) to Cokes (Co-Colas).

We also sold medicines, including Dr. Tichenor's antiseptic. According to a radio ad featuring Cajun Pete, this potion would "make dem mo-skeet bites go down"—but mostly, the liquid went down the hatch, as many farm hands drank it for the alcohol content.

We sold Ramon's Brownie Pills, a "diuretic stimulant to the kidneys," and Ramon's Pink Pills, a "*real* laxative" (no fake laxatives for us!).

To get magic potions and aphrodisiacs, such as King John the Conqueror Root, the farm hands had to go to Tunica, to the City Drug. We didn't do voodoo.

All my commissary clerking was under the tutelage of store manager Tommy Jones, who always wore starched khakis and comported himself with dignity. He was black, but unhesitatingly, and authoritatively, would call a fellow worker "Nigger!" whenever one acted out of line.

Every Saturday there was the same cast, including Deaf Laura (who communicated quite well), Waw (who'd served in World "Waw" II), Flower (noted for smoking some kind of hallucinogenic pig-pen plant, allegedly for asthma), and Candy (who had six fingers on each hand).

When Daddy finished paying off he'd sometimes come out and perform magic tricks such as squeezing a silver dollar into a Coke bottle (the coin was collapsible). The ceiling of the old store, shuttered now, is still dotted with bits of cardboard he'd "tacked" up there by flipping a coin with tack-studded paper wrapped around the coin—after betting newcomers that he could "throw" a tack into the ceiling.

Frivolity was the order of the day.

I felt loved, and I certainly loved these people. They were my extended family. I didn't feel any racial tension then, although I'm sure that some of them would disagree.

Daddy treated the workers with respect. He was honest and could not stand anyone being dishonest with him, dismissing liars with, "You won't do!" I felt the workers respected him.

## Other farm characters

Daddy loved to have fun with characters who peppered the Delta landscape, giving most of them unusual nicknames. For example, I knew of two Coots, not counting one of my aunts.

Coot Lane was noted for rambling around with more possessions than he could carry at one time. Daddy said you could see him coming down the road, but it took him a long time to get where he was going. "He would run up, put his stuff down, then go back and get some more, moving the pile a little farther each time, always saying, 'Jack the bear. Jack the bear.'"

The other Coot was a woman. I once asked her what she was doing, and she replied matter-of-factly, "Standing here talkin' to you." And she was right.

I asked her about a huge knot protruding from her belly. "That's my honey," she replied. It took me a few minutes to realize that it was a hernia.

Willie Duckett, known as Duck, was the closest Daddy ever came to having a foreman. Duck drove his own company pickup truck, which he improved by adding a spinning-knob handle to the steering wheel. The knob featured a blond, naked woman encased in plastic.

## Duck tales

Daddy would send Duck to Tunica on various errands and would often allow me to ride along.

I remember that Duck would often stop at the grocery story and buy a big bunch of bananas, leaving me alone to ogle the steering knob. He would consume four or five bananas on the way back to the farm. Naturally, he was a large man and waddled when he walked.

Duck could barbecue the best ribs I've ever tasted. When I tried to get his recipe, he declined, saying, "I don't have one. I jus' keep tastin' 'til it tastes right."

Daddy told Duck how to test a watermelon for ripeness without even having to thump it, explaining that the secret was looking at the stem, or "curl," on the melon to see if had dried up.

Daddy said Duck responded by saying that, "When your curl's dead, that's it; you'd just as well give up."


## Experts

Before the advent of tractors, Daddy had a head muleskinner, a position he called hostler. He was John Crenshaw and didn't have a nickname, but, when John gave me a black-and-white-checked Dominecker chicken, I nicknamed it Crenshaw. It followed me everywhere, even when I plowed cotton.

But John Crenshaw was no chicken. I remember seeing him at the reins of a wagon with four mules in harness, at full gallop. He popped his bullwhip with deadly accuracy whenever he needed to accelerate. It was a thing of beauty, pure artistry.

His wife, Chris, married Rock Sims when John died, and became Momma's maid, serving faithfully in that job into her old age, until falling over dead at the ironing board one day.

Chris had two granddaughters, named Chontelle and Nicole. Daddy renamed them Shirt Tail and Co' Cola. (Nicknames flourished. Some almost made sense, such as calling Carlester Cholesterol, but other nicknames, like Peepsight and Pump Pipe, were just accepted, without any logical explanation, as far as I knew.)

Another character was a fisherman, Jack Keeley, who ran a set of nets in the lakes between the levee and the river and would often emerge from the woods with fantastic hauls. Sometimes he'd catch alligator snapping turtles weighing about one hundred pounds. He once dumped about twenty live, foot-long terrapins in our sandbox to show off his turtle catch.

He couldn't swim. Whenever his boat capsized, he simply sank to the bottom and walked as far as he could, before shoving himself to the surface periodically to breathe as he "walked" back to the bank.

Another farm hand, Leroy, was an expert in removing wasp nests. I once saw him rub his hands under his armpits, then reach up and pinch a wasp nest off the house with his sweat-soaked hands. The dazed wasps were still clinging to the nest as he gently laid it on the ground and crushed it under his shoe.

We had a yardman named Man (short for Emanuel) who was hard on the wildlife. I saw him kill a mockingbird at twenty paces, throwing a small rock underhanded. I also saw him grab a snake by its tail and sling the outstretched serpent several times around his head before decapitating the snake with a whip-popping motion.

### The Irishman and Boll Weevil

There was one white farmhand when Daddy was growing up. Among my grandparents' four yardmen was Mike, an Irishman who had moved to Tunica County with droves of Irishmen to help dig a three-thousand-foot-long drainage canal (known appropriately as the Irish Ditch), mostly with shovels and wheelbarrows.

It was Daddy's job to summon the yardmen to lunch. Using nicknames for the three black workers, he'd yell. "Zeke-you! Bobby-cue! Molecule!" Then, after a delay, would add, "Mike!"

Mike's reply was consistent: "Quit callin' me with the Negroes!!!!" Of course, Daddy never went along with that request.

Another interesting white character was my cousin, Boll Weevil, who toyed with raising hogs and sheep before renting out his land and leaving farming behind. He dabbled in hypnosis, bought gold before it was commonplace, and learned German before going to Germany to find a bride.

He would often perform a politically incorrect monologue called "Captain Dusty," about the "roughest, toughest, hardest-to-bluffest highway controlman in de Noo Nighted States."

The tale ends when Captain Dusty meets his match, driving up behind a speeder and turning on his "syringe" (patrol-car siren).

"When dat man heared dat wildcat scream, dat man cut his eyes up in dat look-around mirror, stepped on hurry-up, called on so-long, shot three big balls of fire outta de resaust pipe and I swear 'fore God we have not seen him since!"

Some of the blacks were named after whites. When Zeke Thomas named his son Perry Thomas, Daddy threatened to name my youngest brother Zeke, but Momma put her foot down. Now, one of Daddy's great grandsons is named Thomas, so I guess we're all even.

## Leave no stone unturned

Daddy once had to pay a $20 reward and a pair of shoes to the farm worker who found a huge diamond that was lost when Daddy's bunkhouse burned, with Granddaddy's borrowed diamond stickpin inside.

"I offered the reward to whoever could find it," Daddy said, "and Giles Harris walks up, flicks his finger through the ashes about three times, and finds it! The gold had melted, of course, but there was the diamond, shining like it had just come out of a jewelry store."

As far as I'm concerned, the real gems are the characters who dot the landscape of my memory, with names like Plez (short for Pleasant), Gentle, and Darkstuff. I can just flick through the ashes and there they are! They were great people, for the most part.

Daddy's wildest stories live on, thanks to a tape recording he agreed to make one day at his kitchen table.

One tale involved a man named Watt, who was asked to straighten up an attic over my grandparents' garage. He found a huge jug of fruit juice that somehow had developed a leak and fermented. He began sampling the juice, got totally drunk, and was soon seen in the garden, pulling up turnips, tossing them in the air, and yelling to the skies.

Watt wasn't much of a worker and was thought of as a "play-pretty" who often provided comic relief. He once put a live baby pigeon in his mouth, then spit it out.

## Joe Bill

The most colorful tales involve a farm hand named Joe Bill Peters, who liked to hook a mule to his Model T Ford and "drive" around the farm.

Joe Bill was mighty allergic to work, as illustrated by the time Daddy asked him to plant ten peas in a vegetable garden.

"These were special peas that I wanted to grow for seed," Daddy said, noting that they had to be planted just so, spaced properly and at the correct depth. "I dug the holes for him, just to make sure."

It was about ten a.m. when Daddy entrusted the ten peas to Joe Bill, asking him to simply put one pea in each hole and cover the holes with dirt.

After the back-to-work farm bell rang at one p.m., Daddy checked up on his prized worker. "I said, 'Joe, did you get through with them peas?' He said, 'I didn't quite make it. I lacked one pea. I had it outta my pocket and was fixin' to drap it, but the bell rang for twelve, so I stuck it back in my pocket.'"

Daddy said, "Just hand me the pea and I'll plant it myself!"

And that was how Joe Bill reinvented the sharecropping system.


### Unequal shares

Another example of Joe Bill's creativity involved his partnership with the female worker named Coot. "They started a ten-acre cotton crop together," Daddy said, "and, before they even got to chopping time, Joe Bill ran off to Chicago.

"Coot went on through with the crop, gathered the cotton, and, when she settled with me, she made good money."

"One night she saw a masked man at her window. She grabbed her ax and said, 'I'm gone cut yo' head off, if you stick it through that window!'

"About that time the mask fell off and it was Joe Bill. He wanted his half of the crop money! Coot said all he was going to get was his head chopped off."

## "Bee ain't got no snuff!"

Later, Joe Bill got hitched (holding hands and jumping over a broomstick) to a woman known simply as Bee. For a while he seemed to have an earnest interest in taking care of her, as illustrated by the time he flagged down Daddy on the road, looking mighty upset. Daddy stopped his pickup, thinking there might be some medical emergency.

Said Joe Bill, breathlessly, "Bee ain't got no snuff!"

Apparently he thought Daddy would drop everything and make a beeline to the farm store. It didn't work, but the saying—"Bee ain't got no snuff!"—became a family mantra of sorts, uttered randomly when things weren't going just right.

## Self promotion

Next, Joe Bill promoted himself into management—over Bee.

Said Daddy: "Bee flagged me down one day and said, 'I can't chop cotton out here! Every time Joe Bill goes by with the plow he pulls this big old long knife out of a scabbage and waves it at me!'"

Daddy checked and found a ragged, homemade scabbard strapped to Joe Bill's plow handle. In it was a cane knife. "Joe Bill said, 'I was just wavin' it at her to make her hurry up.'"

Daddy took the knife, but soon the arms race escalated. Said Daddy: "One day I saw Joe Bill's Model T with my mule hitched to it. Joe Bill was running 'round it. Then I saw Bee running 'round it, just flying. I went over there and I saw that rascal come out from under the car, then go back up under it real quick. He had a .22 rifle and was trying to hide from me."

Joe Bill's story: "Bee won't do right. I was just scarin' her!"

Daddy confiscated the unloaded rifle, adding it to his arms cache.

Joe Bill really began to lose favor when he showed up for work one morning and began to violently shake one leg of his overalls. Daddy said, "A turd rolled out on the ground! I'm not kidding! I made him go back home."

Much to everyone's relief, Joe Bill soon left the farm for good, and at last report he'd been spotted in Memphis stuffed butt-first into an upright garbage can.

Joe Bill faded into folklore, and new members of the family began to think that maybe he was fictional. Duke's wife, Pam, thought so—until years later her doorbell rang and a man on her doorstep introduced himself as Joe Bill's son.

Pam's jaw dropped and all she could think of to say was, "Bee ain't got no snuff!"

The man had no idea what she was talking about.

## The landscape changes

Soon mechanization reared its head.

At one time Daddy had about one hundred mules, serving some eighty families, counting the ones on land he rented from his sister. The mules were soon replaced with farm machines.

Daddy was deeply saddened when the last mule died.

Apparently some of the workers felt the same way. In his book, *Where I Was Born and Raised,* (Boston: Houghton Mifflin Company, 1948) David Cohn cites an old farm worker who said, "I'd druther have a mule fartin' in my face all day long walkin' de turnrow than dem durned tractors." (pp. 299-300).

Another worker later lamented the advent of all kinds of motorized transport, saying it led to the growing softness of young people, causing back problems that came from "riding on rubber and farting through silk."

Nevertheless, cars had begun to dot our farm, ranging from Joe Bill's mule-drawn Model T to cars that actually ran on their own power. Workers started going off to the nearby town of Tunica on payday.

Eventually Daddy closed his store and we started going to town to watch the passing sidewalk parade on Saturday night. It was always interesting.

My favorite town character was a man who called himself Walk-Low after a train had taken off his legs below the knees. He had an indomitable spirit and wore special backward shoes that fit on his knees and remaining shins, allowing him to earn a living as a stand-up shoeshine artist and comic.

Harold Clanton was the owner of a raucous black juke joint on the edge of town (which was winked at by the local sheriff). Known simply as Hardface, due to his stone-cold poker face, Clanton would cruise through town with not one, but two of the flamboyant chrome spare-tire containers, known as continental kits, mounted on the trunk of his Lincoln.

He was said to be "Tunica's first black millionaire," and was the inspiration for the Bone Face character in Tunica native John Pritchard's ribald novella, *Junior Ray* (Montgomery, AL: NewSouth Books, 2005).

Planter Edgar Hood Jr. tells of a black woman named Walking Rosie who would paint her face white and wander around, sleeping in abandoned tenant houses, and generally scaring the hell out of folks.

One time one of Daddy's farmhands, Rabbit, was caught urinating between two parked cars in town. When he gave his name to police, they asked "Whose rabbit?" Rabbit gave an accurate reply: "Roach's Rabbit!" He was arrested for smarting off, although that was not his intention. Sometimes honesty just doesn't pay.

There was a hefty local farmer who would sometimes corner me on the sidewalk and give me unwanted advice. Later, when I was a teenager, he had four large grain silos alongside Highway 61 painted with giant letters, B-A-R-D, spelling out his first name.

He wasn't too pleased when I went with some friends and changed the "B" to an "L" one night, using silver paint—transforming his name to L-A-R-D.


### A movie star makes the scene

One night I remember seeing Tyrone Power, the movie star, posturing in front of City Drug, smoking his pipe and taking it all in. (He had married a local girl.) I don't know what he was thinking, but to us the Saturday-night scene was better than the movies, and it was free!

No matter what you see in the movies, I believe that many of the workers were happy then, for the most part. Daddy had lots of nostalgic letters confirming this, particularly from workers who had succumbed to the siren song of Dee-troit.

Like many other Delta workers, they filtered onto aortic Highway 61, flowing northward like so many corpuscles headed toward the nation's industrial heart.

Blues legend Robert Johnson was accused of coming to a crossroads and making a deal with the devil, but I think maybe we all made that deal.

When juke joints sprang up in town, Daddy converted a shack into the farm's own juke, appointing head farmhand Duck to run it in an above-board fashion. Daddy didn't profit from the deal, except by keeping the workers away from worse trouble in town or at Hardface's place. "It's better to dance with the devil you know, than one you don't," goes an old saying.

I crawled under the juke one night, but soon got bored with gambling noises. A friend, Bill Gidden, convinced me we'd have more fun under a tenant house on his family's farm. He brought along a medical syringe, which we used to squirt water through floorboard cracks. (The panic in the house subsided after the needle shot through a knothole, giving our game away.)

## Longing for the freedom of one's chains

I fled the farm in my teens, mainly because of asthma (I was allergic to farm work). Still, I can identify with Kris Kristofferson's lyrics in *Loving Arms* about longing for "the freedom of my chains."

One of the farm workers was actually born into chains. Liberated from slavery as a youngster, Jack "Crookleg" Johnson always had a smile and a snaggle-toothed laugh when I visited his home on the farm.

With his signature hearty laugh, he claimed his extremely bowed legs were the result of trying to stop a cannonball during the Civil War. He actually stopped the ball as it gently rolled up to his feet.

He said that before he was liberated as a child, he remembered being fed in a trough. His last name probably came from his former owner (our place originally was known as the Johnson Place) and he was later nicknamed Jack, after the famous prize-fighter Jack Johnson, when a haymow handle hit him upside the head and didn't faze him.

The last time I saw him alive he was over one hundred and was still working in the fields, even after both legs had been amputated. He didn't have to work, he wanted to, dragging himself along down the cotton rows after his wife, Mary, carried him to the fields in a wheelbarrow.

Psychologically, he had chained himself to the land. It must have agreed with him. He lived to 109.

## "America's Ethiopia"

*Not* being there agreed with *me*. I left Tunica County for good when I was fourteen, first going to military school and later roaming the world, then only knowing only that I wanted to be "where I ain't," as one character says in *The Way West* by A. B. Guthrie Jr.

Otherwise, I would have been in Tunica in the 1960s when it was declared the "poorest county in the United States" and in 1985, when Rev. Jesse Jackson came through, ranting about it being "America's Ethiopia."

This was prompted by the fact that some town whites rented rundown houses to blacks along Sugar Ditch, a sewage ditch that ran along one side of town. Our family didn't think the crisis was worth the fuss, since we had our own sewage ditch at the low end of our yard. (However, there were sewage lines in town to which the rental houses could have been connected.)

An information panel at the Tunica Museum says that Rev. Jackson "made two walks the length of Sugar Ditch, trailed by numerous reporters, TV cameras and crowds of supporters." This was followed by a pep rally at a local school gym, where a collection of some $3,700 was made.

"Then Rev. Jackson and his entourage got in their cars and drove away," said Clifford Granbury, former head of the Tunica County School Board. "Neither Rev. Jackson nor the money was seen again in Tunica."

After the story was broadcast, Tunica acquired the Sugar Ditch property, tore down the shacks, and built a forty-eight-unit housing development to replace them. The ditch was lined with cement and enclosed in a steel fence.

Tunica County's population is still mostly black, even though the county lost almost 30 percent of its population during the racial strife of the 1960s.

Many were not bitter. Says the Tunica Museum: "At a reunion of 400 former and Concerned Citizens of Tunica in Kansas City, Missouri, held in 1986, members reflected on their old home in the wake of the focus on Tunica's hardships.

"From doctors and lawyers to businessmen and teachers, they believed that success came because of Tunica—not in spite of it. They looked back on hard times as good times, crediting their success to folks they left behind—parents and teachers who convinced them they could do better—and they did."

One, Charles Tucker, went from cotton picking to working as an agent for professional athletes, including Magic Johnson. The museum quotes him as saying, "Hard work in the fields all day long for zero, from 'I can until I can't,' put me ahead of the rest when I moved to Michigan.

"A hard day's work for me in the North was like a vacation. My grandmother used to work a whole cotton field by herself. My father never missed a day of work. All of that gave me the encouragement I needed. One of the rewards you get in Tunica is better respect for yourself and the insight to do something."

## THE ORIGINAL TRIO

**The Gang of Four**
Robert Cox, Virginia Cox,
Bill Selman, Jett

*Whit, George,
Jett*

**The Three Amigos**
George, Whit, Jack Selman

**The Deck
is Cut**

*Below: 1) Jack, 2) Bill
Gidden, 3) Whit,
4) Sterl Owen,
5) George*

*MEMPHIS JA*

*George, Judy Cox,
Whit, Jack*

*Jack, Whit, George*

*George, Whit, Jack, Duke*

*My "son"
Kubona*

*Jack,
"The Magician"*

*Jack, aka "Bonehead"*

## THE WILD CARDS

# CHAPTER 12

## The Wild Cards

### Shooting the bull

I recently went to Seattle, Washington, to visit with my last remaining aunt, my mother's ninety-two-year-old sister, Bracie.

We reminisced about the past and she told me how she and Momma used to wash the family's clothes in a creek, brush their teeth with sweet-gum branches, and render lard and mix it with potash to make lye soap.

"Making up lies," I claim, fell to her son, my first cousin, Brian Jacobs, when he started telling me about the wonderful summer he spent with us on the farm when we were young boys.

Brian says that one night he and my brother George and I camped out in our clubhouse, located at the foot of the levee behind our house. The entire stretch of levee along Daddy's farm was fenced off with miles of barbed wire and was used as grazing land for his livestock, so the clubhouse basically was inside a vast livestock pen.

Although the fenced-in enclosure was probably a mile long and was sparsely populated with cattle and mules, we woke up to find ourselves surrounded by a concentration of cows—and Daddy's huge Angus bull. Brian said we could smell breakfast cooking, but we weren't hungry enough to run past the bull.

I do remember the bull. Although he was hornless, it didn't deter him from acting bullish when he got horny. I remember him chasing farm hands and often lifting the front of Daddy's truck into the air to prove his strength.

So we devised a plan. George had a pellet gun and fired a shot at the bull's rump, which Brian says failed to move the beast. Brian claims that I bragged, "*I* can move him!"—and proceeded to pump up the air rifle "about twenty-seven times" and shoot him in the testicles.

Brian says the bull took off running toward the farm store, about fifty yards away, where Daddy happened to be standing. Brian says Daddy watched in amazement as the terrified *toro* actually rammed a mule so hard that the innocent four-legged bystander was knocked through the barbed-wire fence.

We made it safely to breakfast, where Daddy wondered aloud, "I wonder what got *into* that bull!" We didn't tell him we'd put some lead in his pencil.

Of course we didn't, as I'm sure this never happened. It's just a bunch of bull as far as I'm concerned.

## Chicken feed

Brian also claims that we later put some leftover July Fourth fireworks to good use, after noticing how the chickens would fight one another when the cook flung the after-dinner table scraps over the chicken-yard fence.

Allegedly, when the cook went inside, we threw lighted firecrackers over the fence and the chickens were running for them—until they started exploding.

Says Brian: "The next time the cook went to feed them she came back into the house puzzled. She said, 'Them's the politest chickens I ever seed!'"

If I get approached by anti-animal-cruelty groups, I'll simply follow the lead of a defendant in a LaGrange, Georgia, court, who recently told the judge, "I stands on the five amendments."

When the judge asked him to explain, he simply said, "It mean I don't have to tell you I stole that car."

And I certainly don't want to do what a masked robber did, when he tried to rob a convenience store in a small Georgia town, where everybody knows everybody. When the clerk asked the robber by name what he thought he was doing, the robber protested: "It ain't me!"

## Wild life

I *do* remember the time George and I went to visit Brian's home in the desert near California's Salton Sea. Brian's father, Bryan Jacobs, had retired from a career as head of what now is the Federal Aviation Authority and was starting an eighty-acre table-grape ranch.

It was so danged hot there that we could chase lizards for only three or four minutes before we'd have to retreat into their air-conditioned house for about twenty minutes.

We finally figured out that nighttime was the best time to play outdoors. Roaming around in the dark with flashlights, we soon discovered that the desert came alive at night.

Having grown up with all kinds of pets in the family—a 'possum named Jim Dandy, a fox named Crabgrass, and a deer named John Deere—I thought this would be an opportunity to expand the menagerie.

When George and I left California, we boarded the plane with a suitcase full of live critters: a snake, a tarantula, a scorpion, assorted lizards, and kangaroo rats. When we got home, only the tarantula and scorpion were alive, and Momma insisted that they become nonliving organisms *fast*!

So, we released the two survivors into the bathtub, hoping they would fight it out and do the job for us. However, they seemed too tired from the trip, so we finally just pickled them both in alcohol. We figured this was all right since they were probably drunk when they died and maybe didn't feel a thing.

Why do young boys do stuff like that? Stuff like little Duke placing frogs in all the boys' suit-coat pockets when Jett had a formal dance at the playhouse?

Steve McQueen's movie character in *The Magnificent Seven* answered it best, when asked why he would want to go up against a superior force of Mexican bandits to save a small village. He explained that he'd known a cowboy in El Paso who once took off his clothes and "jumped in a mess of cactus… He said it seemed like a good idea at the time."

## Bonehead

When I wasn't working on the farm, I really got into devilment when another California cousin, Jack Perry Selman, visited us. Just as Tom Sawyer's life was enlivened by Huck Finn, my boyhood was brightened by this free-spirited tornado of energy, known simply as Bonehead.

My first memory of this rambunctious kid is seeing him running around, naked, outside of Miss Sallie's house, trying to elude Miss Willie Pope, the rotund cook who had been assigned the onerous task of dressing the young boy.

Almost every summer Bonehead, his older brother, Bill, and their mother, my Aunt Ewee, would come to visit for weeks, even months, at a time. We used to count the days until their arrival.

Then, when they'd leave, I'd try to detain them, once warning that there were Germans where they were going. It didn't work. I guess maybe World War II was over by then.

Wars did occur while these cousins were visiting, however. Bill allied himself with my sister and two older cousins, Robert and Virginia Cox, who lived a mile away.

Bonehead allied himself with me and my younger brother, George. They both were about a year younger than I.

I should say that Bonehead allied himself with me *and/or* George, since our alliance broke down quite often. Bonehead always chose the side that was most politically advantageous. Usually this involved food of some sort. (In fact, at lunchtime he would usually compare our fare with Miss Sallie's before deciding where to eat—sometimes simply eating twice.)

When we three weren't getting attacked by the alliance of elders, we found an infinite number of ways to get into trouble.

## Too many Jacks

Bonehead's real name is Jack Perry Selman and, far from being a bonehead today, is an acclaimed Southern California architect. Jack once sold his own self-designed home to movie star Chuck Norris, then built himself an even more spectacular abode.

Since Granddaddy and Daddy were Jacks, we had to come up with a nickname for this cousin, to avoid confusion.

We started out with Jackson, followed by T-Bone Jackson, then T-Bone. Finally Daddy just started calling him Bonehead and the name stuck.

Sometimes it seemed appropriate. For instance, he "borrowed" my cast-iron Elmer Fudd piggybank and gave it to a rich aunt for her birthday. It was a wonderful surprise to our aunt, but more of a surprise to me—and my aunt seemed a little indignant when I got it back from her.

In California, Bonehead also liberated his neighbor's pet rabbits. When forced to return the "borrowed" bunnies and to admit his crime, he simply knocked on the neighbor's door, with Ewee watching from the street, and returned the rabbits, saying, "I found your rabbits."

"Good boy," the neighbor replied.

On another occasion, he tried the truth and it worked. "I stole your pomegranates," he apologized to a neighbor. The neighbor's response was, "That's all right. Take as many as you want."

### Bringing new ideas to The Delta

Mississippi was fertile ground for Bonehead's creativity as he opened avenues of exploration we never had imagined.

Grandmother's huge library, to me, was just a room lined with twelve-foot-tall bookshelves. To Bonehead, this was a mountaineering challenge. He scaled the shelves, inspected the bronze statues of warriors on top, and relieved them of their battle axes.

He dug into books such as *The Works of Rabelais* by Gustave Dore, reveling in passages such as this description of the youthful Gargantua:

"He pissed in his shoes, shit in his shirt, and wiped his nose on the sleeve; he did let his snot and snivel fall in his pottage and dabbled, paddled, and slabbered everywhere."

This was choice stuff for young boys! I had never imagined that the old tomes contained such nuggets of wisdom.

Another favorite place was the blacksmith shop, where George and

I had been content to make things like frog gigs. It became a zip-gun factory when Bonehead arrived.

Once, he taught us how to make intricate model airplanes with balsa wood, glue, and tissue paper. Then, after days of painstaking labor, Bonehead tied a string to his completed plane, set it on fire, and spun the flaming aircraft around and around in the yard, until it crashed. I think he was high on glue.

## Walking on water

Daddy presented Bonehead a long-running challenge. Because Bonehead had such wide feet, Daddy tried to persuade him they were so wide he could walk on water.

This went on for years, with Bonehead protesting vehemently. Finally Daddy offered Bonehead $5 to prove him wrong. A group of family members went with us to a lake in the woods and Bonehead got barefooted and promptly sank in the shallows up to his knees.

Daddy was slow to pay up, claiming that Bonehead had "opened his toes."

## Hell on wheels

When Daddy bought us a Cushman motor scooter, new territory was opened up. One summer we roamed the countryside in the three-wheeled vehicle, taking turns riding in the sidecar, in pursuit of butterflies for a school project for Bonehead's brother Bill. We used old tennis racquets, fitted with nets made from orange sacks.

This nearly killed me. Going about twenty-five miles per hour on a gravel road, I was sitting on the front of the sidecar and lunged for a butterfly overhead. Bill was driving.

My feet hit the gravel road and got dragged under the sidecar, causing me to do a swan dive into the gravel. Next, I got run over and dragged *under* the sidecar. Luckily, I wasn't killed. I only had scrapes over half my body.

When Bonehead, George, and I graduated to Daddy's old army

Jeep, we aimed our sights a little higher than mere butterflies. We "armed" the vehicle with a homemade machine gun, complete with bandoliers of stick bullets held together with Scotch tape. We were after enemy aircraft.

We soon located the enemy, persuading a local crop-duster pilot to ignore his work long enough to go aloft with the bombs we had manufactured in the farm store by filling up small paper bags with corn flour.

## War begins

A former war pilot, the crop duster got in his biplane with the snorting bull painted on the fuselage and took off with his bombs.

With war in full swing, we started driving around on various farm roads, scanning the wild blue for the enemy.

He was nowhere to be seen—until I looked into the rearview mirror and saw a large yellow object bearing down on our tail. The plane was coming right at us, just a few feet above the road, so I veered into a corn field in a desperate escape maneuver.

This wasn't pretend anymore! We heard the biplane's wheels hit the cornstalks as the intrepid pilot banked in our direction and lobbed a bomb right on top of us! Three bombs later, we surrendered. Luckily, Daddy never knew a war had been raging all over the farm.

## Back to abnormal

After that, we went back to fishing and frog gigging. When we found out that a nearby swamp was being drained, we liberated about fifty snakes, bringing them home in a big wooden box—after killing all the poisonous cottonmouths. We were allowed to keep the live snakes for about two seconds after Momma found out.

Once, after a successful frog-gigging trip, Bonehead was watching the cook prepare the frog legs for cooking. The cook explained that she was removing the "leaders," the tendons in the legs. Otherwise, she said, the legs with leaders would react to the heat and possibly jump out of the frying pan.

"How do you know which frogs are the leaders?" Bonehead asked, innocently.

### Over the levee and through the woods

Sometimes we would go on expeditions "over the levee," often traveling through the woods by Jeep for miles along old logging roads to get to the sandbars alongside the Mississippi River.

When the river was very low, there would be huge sand dunes, reminiscent of vast deserts, providing a great place for overnight camping.

One night, in our tent on the dunes, we told each other ghost stories and pretended to be scared. Then we *really* got scared when we saw a mysterious light moving back and forth across the sand dunes.

Luckily, it was only Daddy, tracking us down because some of Bonehead's friends from California had shown up on the farm unannounced.

### On safari

On another trip we let Robert Cox, our older Eagle Scout cousin, join our party.

When he tried to establish himself as our leader, we obligingly fell into a single-file line behind him, holding our guns and gear over our heads like safari porters. After about twenty minutes of getting no more than "Yes, B'wana!" out of us, he finally ceded authority. "Why don't y'all mature?" he barked in frustration.

Frankly, we didn't see any point in it at the time.

On one nighttime coon hunt we let Bonehead do the honors. He shot into the tree, missed the coon, and took out the limb the coon was on. The coon fell to the ground, alive, only to be impaled on the falling limb. We figured that's how it was done in California.

## Girl hunting

As we got older—maturing, finally—we started hunting for girls. That's when we began baiting Bonehead with stories of Irene, a girl we had created for gullible teenage males who might be so unlucky as to breeze in from out of town looking for action.

Here's the way it worked. If the young man's eyes lit up when the "true stories" of a delectable and available Irene were bandied about, then the plot moved to the next level.

"Her dad's out of town tonight," someone would offer excitedly. And that night, if everything went according to script, we'd find ourselves sneaking up on Irene's "house"—really an abandoned sharecropper shack in the middle of nowhere—softly calling, "Irene! Irene! It's *us*."

That was the cue for a co-conspirator to burst out of the shack with a blazing shotgun, yelling, "I done told you 'bout messin' with my daughter!!!"

The idea was to leave the victim stranded, stumbling around in some dark and forlorn cotton field.

When this was tried on Bonehead, it almost backfired. The all-star athlete beat everyone back to the escape vehicle.

To salvage the plan, George pretended to be shot. The Jeep driver roared up to the local hospital emergency room, only to speed off as Bonehead ran toward the building yelling for help.

## Skeletons

A bit of buried history emerged when Bonehead's mom, my Aunt Ewee, died. In his eulogy, Bonehead announced—with Ewee's deathbed blessings—that she had been married *twice* to her first husband.

Ewee had been skewed by scoliosis, but she had a lust for life and grabbed for all the gusto her condition would allow.

As a child, she found herself suddenly without a playmate when all of her older siblings were enrolled in the one-room schoolhouse on the family farm, so she tagged along and began her education at the age of three. Consequently, she graduated from college when she was in her teens.

A young boy, who would later become playwright Tennessee Williams, would often visit the farm with his grandfather, the Rev. Walter Dakin, pastor of the family's Episcopal Church. It was Ewee's job to entertain the boy, since they were about the same age.

But there would be no sparks, since the boy's sexual proclivities pointed in another direction, as the world would later come to know.

(Daddy said he felt that Tennessee's grandfather, Rev. Walter Dakin, also might have been gay. "One time when Mr. Dakin came to visit, Miss Sallie asked me to drive him around the farm. He kept saying over and over that he wanted to see the bulls, one time putting his hand on my leg.")

Ewee eventually began dating Howard Selman, the high school football coach in Tunica, and things progressed so well that they ran off to Arkansas and got married on the sly. After consummating the marriage, they promptly returned home and pretended nothing had happened. Ewee continued to date other people to sell the ruse—until she could wed Howard officially in a family-sanctioned ceremony.

They remained married until Howard's death many years later. She later married another man—but only once.


## The long-lost cousin

Ewee's brother, George Day Perry Jr., had a first marriage that wasn't so successful. Daddy told me that my uncle George's first wife tried to poison him by pouring carbolic acid down his throat as he slept. They split, naturally, and George was left with their daughter, who was reared by Granddaddy Jack and Miss Sallie, her grandparents.

The child turned out to be developmentally impaired, functioning on one level that allowed her even to go to college, but never developing emotionally beyond the level of a child.

One day Grandmomma Sallie left the teenaged girl alone at a Memphis movie theater. When she finished shopping, Grandmomma returned to pick up her granddaughter—and was astonished as the girl gushed about the wonderful man who had "played games" with her in the darkened theater.

The family later initiated a sterilization procedure that rendered my cousin infertile, and she was placed in a home for the mentally impaired in Missouri.

I only met her once, when she visited Miss Sallie. I was only about six and my "lost" cousin was in her twenties. She seemed comfortable playing games on my level. I remember her proudly showing off the basket she had made out of popsicle sticks. It was quite a work of art.

## The ghost cousin reappears

This cousin, Mary Perry, was always referred to as Mary Dent, and most of the later generations didn't even know she existed until one day she showed up, in her eighties, on the old home-place doorstep, now occupied by my brother George's son, George Pace Perry Jr., great-grandson of George Day Perry Sr. (Granddaddy Jack).

Mary had gotten one of her custodians to drive her there, looking for her grandparents, and couldn't seem to readily grasp that the current occupant was generations removed from the George she was hunting.

She was invited into the house and gave the occupants a historical tour. "This is where Grandmomma sat. This is…"

Before leaving, she ended up with the phone numbers of many of her first cousins and for many months thereafter, until she died, she made up for lost time, bombarding us with juvenile phone calls.

Her end of the conversations rarely rose above this level: "Which hand do you wipe with? Your right hand? I use toilet paper myself."

She was proficient in reciting silly poems.

I always tried to listen as patiently as possible, but I finally asked her to limit her calls to once a week.

My brother George even made a trip to Missouri to visit her.

Sadly, she died never having been invited to a family reunion. Shame on us!

## Monkeying around

Because there are so danged many cousins, our Perry family reunions are crowded events. Somehow, at Ewee's request, I got appointed to head up the entertainment, along with Bonehead.

I guess we were the natural choices since we don't mind making monkeys of ourselves. Maybe this stems from the fact that Daddy almost added a real chimpanzee to our family.

This was back when one of the first network-television talk shows featured a chimpanzee named J. Fred Muggs, and Daddy decided he *had* to have his own chimp.

It never happened; I guess personal apes were hard to come by in those days. But that was all right—because Daddy soon had Duke, my younger brother.

My other brother, George, and I had reached about nine and ten, respectively, and were much too old for Daddy to drag along with him when he drove to town for the mail or farm supplies.

So Duke became Daddy's newest little sidekick at the tender age of three. They were inseparable and had their own little vaudeville shtick, performed at the drop of a hat at the barbershop, post office, or anywhere there was a captive audience. Here's a sample:

Daddy—"Duke, what's a bad word?"
Duke—"Darn ain't no bad word?"
Daddy—"Well, what IS a bad word?"
Duke—"Doodoo."

Daddy and the Amazing Talking Boy were a hit.

## The dancing duo

George and I loved this turn of events the most, because it let us off the hook. Just a few years earlier we'd had the pleasure of dancing on plantation backroads for all of Daddy's farm hands.

That was because Momma, bless her heart, had perhaps seen one too many Fred Astaire movies and just *had* to drive forty miles to

Memphis almost every Saturday so that our sister Jett could get on the fast-track to stardom at the Mary Lee Edwards Dance Studio.

If Momma had been smart she'd have left George and me at home on the farm. But, noooooooo....

Mary Lee Edwards soon grew tired of the two little boys who occupied themselves with creative endeavors such as running across the tops of cars, so she persuaded Momma to add two more pupils to her class.

And, boy, did Mary Lee get revenge! She devised a scheme which had George and me singing "Bongo, Bongo, Bongo, I don't wanna leave the Congo, Oh no, no, no, no!"—while tap dancing in top hats and tails. We even had little canes.

Being a good businessman, Daddy figured he'd get his money's worth by taking the show on the road; so that's how we ended up kicking up dust in turn-rows all over the old plantation, performing before droves of cotton choppers.

Yeehaa! Management was adding a fringe benefit: on-the-job entertainment!

(Unfortunately, Daddy didn't pay us for this work, but he did hand out quarters to various farm workers when they'd respond by dancing when he'd ask them to "Hit that step!" One woman found a way to raise the payout to fifty cents by going up to her house and literally hitting the front steps.)

### The show must *not* go on!

I put an end to our fledgling dance careers when George and I were scheduled to perform in Memphis at the MidSouth Fairgrounds. When our time on the recital program came, I refused to budge. Mary Lee figured that if she shoved George out onto the stage that I'd follow—which I did, long enough to drag George back offstage.

Mother finally gave up. George and I soon began learning to plant, plow, chop, and pick cotton. Free at last, we thought (erroneously, we later realized, when the novelty wore off).

## Enter the Duke of The Delta

That's when Duke came along.

Daddy enjoyed making up stories for Duke, particularly his own Jimmy Turtle stories. One day Daddy decided to persuade Duke that there were barnacles living in the woods between the Mississippi River and the levee. To make the story convincing, he'd take Duke out on the acres of sandbars along the river and show him "barnacle tracks"—usually bird footprints or some mysterious trails left in the dunes by windblown leaves.

Then, back in town, he'd let Duke go on and on, warning the general populace of the barnacle threat.

So Daddy didn't get a chimpanzee, but he did enjoy making monkeys of his boys.

## We monkey with Mother Nature

That may explain why George, Bonehead, and I, during our adolescent tree-climbing phase, once went to bed with gloves on our feet. We crossed our fingers and prayed earnestly that God would grant us monkey feet. We were shocked when we woke up with human feet.

Resigned to my fate, I got a set of nine-inch nails and began hammering a spike into the biggest cottonwood tree in our yard. It stuck out five inches and was two feet off the ground.

My plan was to make a nail ladder up the tree to accommodate my human feet. However, driving the first nail took so much energy I decided I'd wait for the tree to grow upward, lifting the nail as it grew; then, I'd nail another and another as my ladder grew skyward.

For years I waited patiently as the lone nail, still two feet off the ground, slowly was engulfed by the tree.

It didn't grow up. But I did. Somewhat.

## God throws me a bone

I figured the next best thing would be to own a gorilla suit like the one I'd seen in an Abbott and Costello movie. Each Christmas, for years, I put gorilla suit at the top of my wish list.

Alas, God had failed me, and now Santa followed suit.

Now, in my old age, God has seen fit to throw me a bone.

Having heard the gorilla-suit story, my son Rob has donated $50 in my name to the Dian Fossey Gorilla Fund International. On my den wall proudly hangs a photograph of little Kubona, my own adopted mountain gorilla son!

Dance, Kubona, dance! You don't have to leave the Congo!

I'm one happy silverback!

With Holiday Inns founder,
Kemmons Wilson

# J WHITLEY PERRY
*"WHIT" ~ "J WELLINGTON" ~ "WHITTICUS" ~ "DADDY" ~ "POPS"*

# CHAPTER 13

## The Turn

### A very different Hollywood ending

I turned my back on our home in The Delta at an early age, mostly for health reasons. I was shipped off to boarding school at fourteen, then worked summers in the Caribbean, teaching spearfishing and scuba diving. This summer work continued throughout my college career, which was interrupted by an around-the-world trek.

Now that I'm long removed from The Delta, I often wonder what it was like when Old Man River was able to get out of bed and walk around, unimpeded by levees. He left behind long, curved scars when he retreated. These old riverbeds streak the landscape today.

One of these is McKinney Lake, named after an old Scots Indian. It runs between the old home place and Hollywood

Just west of Hollywood, McKinney Lake fans out into a cypress brake, an eerie bayou filled with cypress "knees," those knotty spikes that thrust up several feet from the roots between the towering cypresses.

One old timer reports that he could remember seeing my grandmother being helped along the tracks to catch the train after being rowed for several miles across the bayou.

Miles away, on its other end, McKinney Lake butts up against the foot of the levee, where a pumping station eventually was built to transfer excess water back across the dam.

### The bridge to the future

Eventually a bridge was built across Kinney Lake, as it came to be known, so that farmers could drive their wagons around the treacherous bayou to Hollywood or Tunica, a few miles to the south.

When I was a boy, the bridge was a wood and steel contraption with a roadbed of crisscrossed boards to support wagons or cars.

One of my favorite pastimes was to stand on the bridge and watch the passage of wildlife below, including huge snakes, six-foot-long alligator gars, and primitive-looking soft-shelled turtles as big as car tires. The water was relatively clear, compared to the muddy mess that it is now.

Some Sundays the banks at the base of the bridge would be lined with white-robed blacks participating in a singing, hand-clapping baptism ceremony. Some of those being dunked often got held under a dangerously long time, I guess because they had a lot of sins to be washed away.

I loved it when Daddy would let me ride with him to get the mail in Hollywood. The gravel road along the brake always had critters crossing it, usually snakes, large wayward turtles known as cooters, and smaller musk turtles known as stinkin' jims. Occasionally we'd be treated to a weasel, mink, fox, or bobcat darting across the road in an effort to get back to the swamp.

We picked up the mail at Joe Turnage's general store, which featured an ambulatory two-legged terrier who had lost a battle with a train. Daddy would treat me to a bag of pork rinds or vanilla wafers for the trip back home.

Daddy would tell me stories such as the time he was going home from Hollywood in a small mule-drawn carriage: "I was near home, in a hurry, and I got to whipping him so hard, he kicked up his hind legs and got them caught up in the rigging, so I just let him go on home on two legs."

He said his brother, Toby, once came home from Hollywood with a huge keg of crackers. "He liked saltines, and when he got home he had so many in his mouth he was blowing cracker crumbs all over the place," Daddy said. "Miss Sallie made him take all those crackers back and trade them in for a can of tomatoes."

One day Daddy and I stopped along the railroad tracks and watched the gandy dancers, a railroad crew of about eight black workers and a white foreman. The workers' job, to straighten and align the tracks, was accomplished by placing steel pry bars along the rails.

Each man would work his pry bar back and forth to the rhythm of a work chant, and on the last note of the chant all the workers would give a huge heave, shouting in unison. It was a thing of beauty. It moved the tracks and it moved me.

## Death creeps into The Delta

Our mail was simply addressed with our names and "Hollywood, Mississippi." Zip codes came later, as did a new concrete bridge, asphalt roads, and the agricultural poisons that would put an end to the bounty of the bayou—moving up the food chain and wiping out almost everything else, from the cawing crows to the silent, circling buzzards.

At first, pesticides were distributed by mule riders who employed hand-cranked devices. Eventually Daddy bought a High Boy, a tall, twin-tanked, engine-driven rig that could be driven through tall crops, spraying herbicides, insecticides, and, at picking time, defoliants that caused the cotton to drop its leaves, so that it could be picked more easily.

Eventually the job would be done with airplanes, aided by a spotter on the ground, who innocently served as a marker and got dusted with poison or defoliant on each pass.

Before the advent of modern cotton-picking machines, an experimental mule-drawn affair was co-invented by my uncle Frank Perry, who later became an oil-industry engineer. The machine basically was a large vacuum cleaner on a motorized wagon, with octopus-like arms radiating out to men who would walk alongside, sucking up the cotton into bags through the hoses.

## Progress gets the sack

My grandfather quickly gave up on it, going back to the long, snaking, cotton-picking sacks that farm hands had been dragging through the fields for years. When pickers had filled their sacks they'd drag them to one of the tin-roofed cotton houses that dotted the fields.

They'd weigh the sack, have the weight recorded by a manager, and then dump the cotton inside the small hut, to be picked up later and taken to a cotton gin, where it would be stripped of seeds, baled, and shipped to market.

The job of picking was brutal, with the dried spikes of the open bolls sometimes making your hands bleed—until you had built up the proper calluses.

When my brother, George, and I had our first cotton crop, we reveled in tilling, planting, and sowing behind a mule, geeing and hawing to our hearts' content.

We were not exhilarated by the chopping process, walking up and down endless, dusty rows to first thin the cotton, then coming back time after time, removing weeds with a hoe—without removing the cotton stalks.

## We go into management

Since we *really* didn't cotton to the picking process, we soon devised a plan. We were so young that Daddy felt it prudent to have a mammy, our beloved Chris, nearby to supervise us. "This is fun," we told her. She knew better, but she pitched in anyhow, knowing that we were in over our heads.

Enjoying the perks of "management," I snatched some time off to lie in the high cotton atop my little cotton sack and "read" *National Geographic.* I was interested in anthropology, particularly as depicted by photos of topless native women.

It was then that I began to plant the seeds of escape—my bridge to another way of life.

## When one door closes

Daddy always tried to convince me that, with asthma, I should seek a profession other than farming. He had no suggestions, except to say that he would support any decision I might make and would send me to the appropriate schools.

I started my education at Tunica Elementary School, where my first-grade teacher, called Aunt Clara, maintained discipline by tying miscreants to their desk chairs and taping their mouths shut. Needless to say, there were few discipline problems after the first week or so, except for ongoing surliness by one over-aged, overall-wearing student.

I progressed through the system with an eclectic mix of students, all Caucasian, except for one overage Chinese boy, Wong Lum. Daddy called him One Lung. Wong was very polite and was amazing at math, sometimes using an abacus and amazing us with his dexterity with the ancient calculating instrument.

Almost every Delta town had at least one Chinese family—holdovers from a failed attempt to use them as farm laborers. Most ran grocery stores catering to the black trade, usually handing customers a stick to point out what they wanted to buy.

Two of the Lum children are named after Charlie and Ruby Cargile, Tunicans who successfully lobbied for the admission of the Chinese students into the previously all-white schools

In the upper grades there were two Tong boys from Robinsonville who were excellent football players.

One classmate, Bridget Costello, was the daughter of Pat Costello, a Gypsy king who owned a local mule business. It was said that Mr. Costello could not read or write, but he could remember every mule he had sold, even telling you when you bought it and what you paid.

Bridget was a good student but disappeared in her early teens, and was said to have been "married off" to another Gypsy.

Some of the most interesting kids were from Little Texas, a nearby community of white farm workers. They would bring their own homemade toys to school, including spinning tops and wire puzzles. The craftsmanship was brilliant.

In the third grade I got put in a special class for slow students until my parents finally figured out my problem was nearsightedness. I was fitted with glasses and was restored to my previous class, having totally missed out on multiplication table lessons.

The teaching was hit or miss. My fifth-grade teacher once spent a morning telling us about the time a flying saucer landed in her yard.

She later must have been transported into space; she disappeared after only one year.

## Another door opens

I poured myself into my studies and, at fourteen, I found myself in Chattanooga, Tennessee, in a McCallie School military uniform, alone among strangers—and in *way* over my head. I was skinny, undersized, bespectacled, and asthmatic.

I was saved by Frank Gall, a North Carolina upperclassman who took it upon himself to be my guardian. He called me Little One. Building on his kindness, I made it through the first year of hazing in good shape.

Since land plays such an important role in this book, I should note that there was another upperclassman of note at McCallie at the time—future billionaire Ted Turner, who now owns millions of acres of land in eleven states and Argentina.

I admire Ted for his environmentalism. His biggest land holdings are in New Mexico, Nebraska, Montana, and South Dakota. He has more than fifty thousand bison. He has encouraged prairie dogs to flourish, and reintroduced swift foxes and cutthroat trout. He also wants to restore the black-footed ferret.

He has formed foundations to protect the environment, stabilize the world's population, and stop nuclear-arms proliferation.

Although he would come under fire for labeling Christianity a "religion for losers," Ted offered the very religious McCallie School a very large donation. The Presbyterian school had no difficulty in taking it.

Approaching seventy, Ted has mellowed, and, according to a 2007 article in the *Atlanta Journal-Constitution*, claims to be neither agnostic nor atheistic, even praying for sick friends because "it doesn't hurt."

## My health improves

In my sophomore year at McCallie I was joined by my lifetime best

Tunica friend, Sterl (Sterling W. Owen III).

Because I was so homesick my first year, Daddy also sent my brother, George, to the school. "I was supposed to keep Whit company," George would later say, "but I hardly ever saw him."

My last three years at McCallie flew by without much strife. I grew considerably, bulked up, and lettered on the track and swimming teams.

I could probably climb the gym rope faster than anyone in the school, and was dubbed Rhesus as a salute to my simian abilities. A pole vaulter, I tied for second place in the annual Mid-South prep school competition.

My health really got a boost after the school was visited by the owner of a boys' spearfishing summer camp in the Caribbean. He was recruiting campers. Daddy thought it might help me and agreed to let me go.

## Aqua boy

When I was fifteen, I boarded a plane to Atlanta and joined a group of campers for an island-hopping adventure aboard small planes that landed throughout the Caribbean, ending up on the tropical island of Tobago, just off the coast of Venezuela.

The camp was started by Bill and Ann Petry, of my current home city of LaGrange, Georgia, who named it Camp Crusoe, since the fictional Robinson Crusoe was stranded on a fictitious island modeled after Tobago. Bill and Ann had honeymooned on the island after a *Pageant* magazine article proclaimed it was one of three unspoiled paradises left on earth.

They had been recreation majors at Florida State University, intent on starting a youth camp somewhere. When they fell in love with Tobago, the seed was planted for a spearfishing camp there, and they began recruiting at various boys' schools, focusing on swim team members.

Bill's uncle, Atlantan Gardner Allen, had put them up to it, encouraging them to see some of the world while they were young.

I attended Camp Crusoe for six summers, working my way up from camper to counselor to director. I really liked Uncle Gardner and Bill and Ann Petry, who became like a second set of parents to me. (The Petrys are the reason I later moved to LaGrange, where they have now retired.)

## In the swim of things

At Camp Crusoe we were in the water almost every day, usually spearfishing with snorkels or exploring reefs in scuba gear. Breathing air that had filtered across the Atlantic from Africa allowed me to live without a handkerchief at the ready for the first time in my life. Constantly holding my breath built up my lungs, and eventually I outgrew my asthma and was able to free-dive about seventy feet, I'd guess.

Every day in the water brought some new adrenaline rush, such as swimming into the "eye" of a vortex of hundreds of circling barracudas or swimming with giant manta rays.

Brushes with sharks occurred often, but usually posed little danger. One took a fish off my spear, but I had not felt personally threatened. The main trick was not to stay in one place too long after drawing blood. We moved from reef to reef daily.

## "Jaws" strikes

However, one day while spearfishing and searching for a wounded fish, I glanced behind me in time to see what seemed to be a small fish in the distance, heading straight toward me. Suddenly, what I had thought was a mackerel had morphed into a frenzied eight- or ten-foot shark (I didn't measure). I spun around in time to get the spear point between me and this incoming torpedo of gnashing teeth.

For an eternity—lasting perhaps only minutes—the agitated shark lunged as I parried. Squirming and grunting, I was doing my best to build an impenetrable wall with that tiny spear point.

I was afraid to shoot, for fear of disarming myself in case this shark had buddies more loyal than mine (mine had gotten into the boat).

With each lunge, the shark would come about an inch from the spearpoint and retreat.

Then he tried something new. He began to circle. And, for the first time, I had the chance to do more than grunt through my snorkel. I yelled for the boat, not even taking my head out of the water long enough to complete that one syllable.

As I yelled, he was lunging again, but the noise seemed to confuse him. He made two larger, swooping circles, and disappeared. I was swiveling my head around like the girl in *The Exorcist*, trying to relocate him, when suddenly our whaler rowboat pulled alongside.

I lifted myself into the boat with one arm, almost going over the other side and dragging the loaded spear-gun behind, in violation of a rule. "You forgot to unload your gun in the water," chided one of the deserters.

Malcolm, our big brawny boatman, began laughing. "You've turned white, *mon!*" I don't think I grinned back. For the next few days I focused rather intently on the "land activities" part of my job description.

I had been offered a year-round job at the camp and suddenly it didn't seem so attractive.

### Changing lives, one boy at a time

Camp Crusoe changed a lot of lives many ways. A couple of boys joined the crew of the University-Afloat, a windjammer classroom for young adventurers, then bought their own boat and sailed around the world on their own, followed by another around-the-world trip with their wives (one marriage survived).

Another got a job on a ship and was shipwrecked in the Pacific, washing up alive on the island of Raratonga. One now owns a coffee plantation in Central America.

Another, Robert Schwab III of Atlanta, made world headlines when he single-handedly sailed from the Philippines to Vietnam, when it was still hostile to Americans, in a failed Rambo-like attempt to liberate a girlfriend. He was held captive for sixteen months, on suspicion of spying, before being released.

It was Uncle Gardner Allen, as we all called him, who encouraged me to see the world, when he noticed I was moping around trying to figure out what I wanted to do with my life. I was a junior at Vanderbilt University and had no clue where my life was headed.

"You're young," he said. "Go see the world."

And that's exactly what I did. I went all the way around the world, hitchhiking wherever possible.

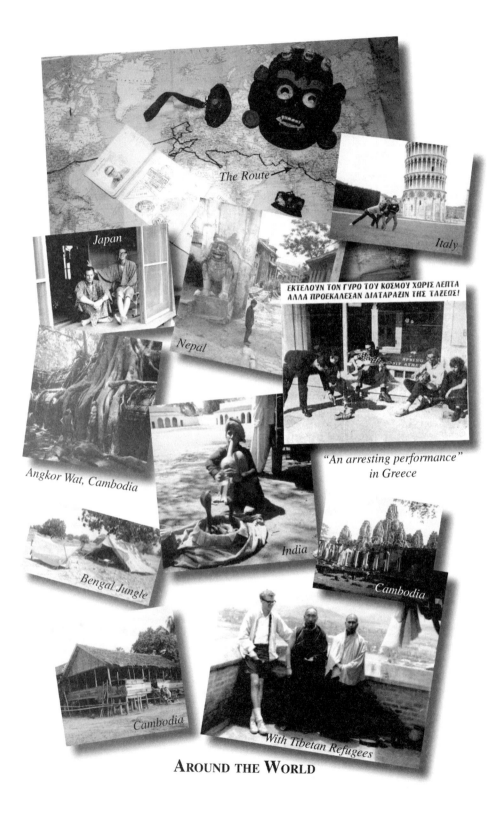

The Route

Italy

Japan

Nepal

ΕΚΤΕΛΟΫΝ ΤΟΝ ΓΥΡΟ ΤΟΥ ΚΟΣΜΟΥ ΧΩΡΙΣ ΛΕΠΤΑ
ΑΛΛΑ ΠΡΟΕΚΑΛΕΣΑΝ ΔΙΑΤΑΡΑΞΙΝ ΤΗΣ ΤΑΞΕΩΣ!

Angkor Wat, Cambodia

"An arresting performance"
in Greece

India

Bengal Jungle

Cambodia

Cambodia

With Tibetan Refugees

**AROUND THE WORLD**

# CHAPTER 14

## Shuffling
---

### Go east, young man, go east!

There's a swirling skein of leaves chasing its tail across the Blue Ridge Parkway. It's autumn and the dry foliage is falling as the trees draw in their sap to fight the coming cold.

I'm in my sixties, on the cusp of winter, and I can feel my own sap waning. The stereo in my car is blaring out Bob Seger's coming-of-age song of lust, *Night Moves*, and while I can still vaguely identify with the song's youthful rawness, the ending lyrics haunt me.

As the song's tempo slows to a crawl, an older and wiser Seger talks about waking to the sound of thunder and wondering how far off it is. "Started hummin' a tune from 1962," he says. "Funny how the night moves with autumn closin' in!"

I'm driving alone in mid-October, a few miles southwest of Asheville, enjoying the peak autumn color of the North Carolina mountains, when suddenly the cold, gray clouds close in and visibility fades to about ten feet.

I've just left my fortieth Vanderbilt University class reunion in Nashville—"Class of '63," another gathering of gray. I find myself enveloped in a fogbank of memory.

I didn't graduate with my class (it was a year later) because in 1962 and 1963 I was contemplating my navel. At twenty-one I went to Europe in search of Truth.

### The kings of the Queen Mary

I withdrew $800 from my savings account and, after taking a Greyhound bus to New York City (where I was too terrified to come out of my room at the YMCA), I crossed the Atlantic aboard the old Queen Mary, crammed into a small cabin with a guitar-playing New Yorker, an Oregonian who was on his way to a backpacking trip down the length of the African continent, and a Hindu on his way back to India.

One night a songfest called a "hootenanny" broke out in one of the lower-class lounges. I got my guitar and joined in. I played almost every Kingston Trio song I knew and soon I was friends with dozens of other young college-age kids. I even had my own groupie, a beautiful young thing who hung on my arm when I wasn't playing.

It was then that I met three young men from Sacramento, California, who invited me to throw in with them when we got to Paris. My new buddies were Patrick Ardell, R. D. Chapman, and Steve Downey. We had a blast.

One night R. D., who was a pretty good gymnast, joined me on deck for some stupid exercises. We were bounding around, swinging on cables, and the next thing I knew R. D. was over the railing, dangling over the ocean, hanging by his hands. He had done it on purpose and was laughing in the face of certain death.

He hoisted himself back over the railing, onto the deck, and promptly fell and broke his wrist!

## Back on dry land

We reached Paris without further incident and spent a few days seeing the major sites, walking miles through the astounding art-filled Louvre and climbing to the top of the Eiffel Tower.

Next we rented a Volkswagen bus, splitting the cost four ways. On many nights this became our hotel. We slept in it and under it many times. We also used a book called *Europe on $5 a Day* to periodically find cheap lodgings, mostly in youth hostels, when we needed baths.

We meandered across France to Switzerland, where we entertained ourselves in one castle by performing our own sword fights in the dining hall.

We then went to Munich, Germany, where the beer was flowing during Oktoberfest. The Cuban Missile Crisis came and went, and we were oblivious to the fact that the world was on the brink of nuclear war. We were "in the moment," trying to "out-Jack Kerouac," as Pat Ardell would later say.

We next dropped down into Austria, where our activities ranged from attending a symphony to driving right up to the Iron Curtain and peering into Communist Czechoslovakia. We could see the sunlight glaring off the rifle scopes as they checked us out. It was eerie.

We then headed to Italy, where we toured Venice, with its fabled canals, before driving to Florence. Arriving at night, we pulled into a Florentine lover's lane by mistake.

We were snoring away in the bus, only to be awakened by a puzzled policeman, who perhaps was trying to catch lovers in the act.

I think that when daylight came and we saw that the ground was paved with used condoms, my friends' testosterone levels kicked into overdrive. They wanted to head to the beaches, wherever they were.

I begged them to take the time to at least see Michelangelo's *David*. I got outvoted.

## I Google a ghost

Recently I Googled Patrick Ardell's name, and, lo and behold, I found that my old friend is a professional artist living in the New York City area, painting under the name El Drecko, a play on the famous artist, El Greco.

This came as a great surprise to me. We established an e-mail connection and Pat explained that at the time we were traveling together he had not yet developed a passion for art.

"You were hip to culture," he replied. "We were from a land of lawn mowers, sprinklers, and strip malls."

However, he said, "We somehow found our way to the Louvre, El Greco's house in Spain, and the Met in Amsterdam."

Returning to Sacramento, Pat enrolled in Sacramento State and got a BA degree. "I was, of course, advised against attempting to make it as an artist, a painter," he said. "But Europe's influence was too great."

Facing a defining moment, he asked what his life would be like as a painter. "There was only one way to find out: live it, painting when others were getting up to go to work, painting on Friday night and missing the party, painting instead of getting that great job and having all the nice things, the SUV, the vacations, the house and the kids, birthday parties, sleepy kisses, picnics in the park on the Fourth of July."

Isn't the Internet amazing! Heck, I might even be able to find myself!

## Beaches? What beaches?

After visiting Rome (where we were unable to find beaches and had to settle on the Vatican and all the major archaeological wonders), we went to Spain, then returned to Paris and got rid of our rented bus.

We split into pairs and began hitchhiking. R. D. and I traveled together, after I bought an old army pack for a dollar in a flea market and shipped everything back home except two changes of clothes and my guitar.

We caught rides through Belgium, the Netherlands, and West Germany. We walked across Checkpoint Charlie into the Communist sector of Berlin, where we spent a day nervously looking around, hoping we could get back out, which we did.

When we arrived in Copenhagen, Denmark, R. D. reconnected with a Danish girl he had met on the Queen Mary. We then met up with the other two hitchhikers and my three friends headed home, leaving me alone. By this time I was street smart and felt comfortable alone.

## Off the wall

I caught a Danish freighter across the North Sea to Scotland.

The captain invited me to his smorgasbord table, but I was unable to eat a bite, due to seasickness. Europe was experiencing its worst winter in twenty years, I was told, and I believed it, the way the ship was lurching along. One time it tipped over so far that I rolled off my bunk onto the wall, then off the wall onto the bunk again.

At last I arrived in Newcastle, Scotland, where I was looking forward to conversing in English again. I asked an old Scot for directions and I still have no idea what he said.

I didn't have much more luck when I hitched a ride with an Englishman. Finally, I figured out that he was trying to tell me that his tongue (and his testes) had been cut out by the Nazis. He managed to tell me about three of his comrades being shot by a seven-year-old girl, whom he killed with his bare hands.

In Edinburgh I stayed in a YMCA, where one day the manager evicted a rough-looking, kilt-wearing Scot, then yelled that he had stolen her purse. With the aid of another young man, I ran the suspect down, tackled him, and hauled him back into the office, where the "stolen" purse had been found. Oh well. It's not every day you get to tackle a man in a dress.

At the YMCA I met up with an American, Bob Lenz of Gloversville, New York. We joined forces and hitchhiked together to London. We had to take the subway for the last few miles, only to find that the city was engulfed in smog and the subways were packed.

We finally got off and struggled to the London streets, where visibility was only about two feet. I had a serious asthma attack, but managed to survive, unlike more than 150 Londoners who, according to news reports, died directly from the smog or in smog-related accidents.

## God save the queen a seat

We secured some cheap lodgings and waited for the air to clear. When it did, we were able to see the Queen of England as she entered a theater for the grand opening of *Lawrence of Arabia*. I was amazed at how small she appeared.

We saw the movie the next day. Over the next week we hit all the main tourist attractions. I then parted with my friend and crossed the English Channel to Paris, where I was able to connect with my cousin, George "Jack" Wilson Perry. He was an American oil-company executive, in charge of drilling in North Africa.

He and his wife, Pat, invited me to spend the Christmas holidays in their palatial three-story home on the outskirts of Paris, at Seine et Oise. I hope I repaid them by helping their nanny with their four young children, Sallie, Susan, Annie, and Tobe. We had a lot of fun, singing folk songs. No Elvis.

When I broached the idea of not going home, but going east to see the rest of the world, my cousin was very supportive. "Heck," he joked years later, "I thought you were never going to leave!"

### I light out alone

After New Year's Day he put me on a train, headed south to Madrid, Spain.

I never will forget looking out the window of the moving train, in southern France or northern Spain, and seeing a man walking in the snow across a white farm field with a shotgun in his hands, presumably hunting rabbits. I had hunted rabbits in the snow at home. Suddenly the world felt smaller and I felt right at home.

In Madrid I lived for a month in a *pensione,* a type of boarding house. My private room was only a dollar a day, including three full meals!

I spent days reading *TIME* magazine from cover to cover, taking Spanish lessons, trading English lessons for Flamenco guitar lessons, and going to bull fights. At night I went to bars, once bumping into my old England hitchhiking buddy, Bob Lenz.

Finally I decided on a trip strategy. I gave up trying to wait out the cold weather and started hitchhiking toward Barcelona. I made it quite a ways, but because the landscape was covered with snow, I eventually broke down and caught a train for the rest of the trip. By this time I was carrying two guitars, having bought a beat-up old Flamenco model in Madrid.

### Asea

I caught a freighter in Barcelona and sailed to Marseilles and Nice, France, then Naples, Italy, where we stopped over long enough for a trip to Mount Vesuvius and the amazing ruins of Pompeii. We then headed south to Alexandria, Egypt, where I caught a ride in a Mercedes with a wealthy Egyptian businessman. We drove south to Cairo as the Sahara sands blew across the road.

Another passenger was a "colored" South African Muslim, who agreed to share a room with me in a cheap hotel on a backstreet. We got up each morning and he bowed to Mecca in prayer before we headed out to see Cairo. When he left to go home, I stayed, eating alone in the local restaurants.

One day Paul Emorphiadis, a young Greek, came up to me in a small café and asked if I was lost. When I told him I was there by choice, he invited me to join him and his friend, Isaac, a Palestinian refugee. They had been playing backgammon at another table.

I struck up a friendship and joined them every day for a week, meeting more and more of their friends each day. I found out that Paul's mother had come to Egypt to sew Elizabeth Taylor's costumes for the movie *Cleopatra*. They had stayed in Cairo so Paul could avoid the military draft in Greece.

### "I'm not an American"

Paul and Isaac took me under their wings, teaching me how to say "I'm not an American" in Arabic (*ana mush Amrikany*) so the shoeshine boys would quit running up to me, stomping on my canvas shoes, and asking, "Shine?"

They hooked me up with some Jordanian students, Salem, Subhi, and Khalil, who were feasting in celebration of the end of fasting day. I joined in with them, eating the rice-and-camel-milk meal with my fingers. Once I forgot, and used my left hand. This is a no-no since they reserve their left hand for sanitary purposes.

Luckily for me, they simply ate around the spot where my left hand had touched. I was embarrassed!

The worst thing that happened to me on the entire trip happened in Egypt, when I let a stranger take me on a tour of the pyramids. He borrowed a dollar from me, then borrowed my address book to allegedly write down his new address. He simply marked through his "old" address and I never got my dollar back. His name, Moheb Mohammed, is still in the little book.

I left Egypt aboard a freighter headed for Greece. I was riding deck class, which means I didn't have a cabin—a poor choice, since it snowed while we were crossing the Mediterranean.

## Shoe business

In Athens I thawed out at a local youth hostel.

I am amazed today by Greece's ability to pull off their recent Olympic games with a minimum of disruption, because, back in 1963, the Athens police seemed intent on creating their own disruption, at my expense.

My alleged crime prompted a local newspaper cartoonist to draw a picture of me taking money from the prime minister of Greece.

At my hostel I met up with a British guitar player and, just for kicks, we strolled down to Constitution Square one day to strum a few folk songs. It just seemed like the thing to do, since Greece is the cradle of democracy. Maybe freedom of speech wasn't included.

We were enjoying ourselves immensely, when suddenly a crowd began forming. To our amazement, people began throwing money at our feet. "We need a can or something," I said, removing one of my Converse canvas shoes. Soon it was full of cash!

As the crowd grew bigger, a photographer emerged, took our picture, and disappeared. We surmised later that he probably had reported us to police, to enhance the value of his photos.

A uniformed officer arrived and began spouting something that seemed to anger the crowd. A little old Greek lady started banging the policeman over the head with a bouquet of flowers.

I used to joke that I knew every song except Greek ones. When somebody would ask me to then play something I didn't know, I'd simply shrug and say, "That's Greek to me!"

The lady with the bouquet could have been yelling, "We don't have enough toiler paper or infrastructure to ever be able to host the Olympics!" It was all Greek to me.

Undaunted, the policemen nudged us in the direction of the local police department.

## Catch and release

Then, in a burst of inspiration, one of our British girlfriends whipped out her harmonica and began blowing the "Colonel Bogey March."

If you've experienced the movie *The Bridge on the River Kwai*, you've heard this tune, which the British prisoners whistled to annoy their Japanese captors as they marched defiantly to their forced labor.

The crowd picked up on this instantly and began whistling, marching defiantly behind us all the way to, and into, the police station—causing the constabulary great consternation. Reluctantly, the dejected officers let us go without pressing charges.

That was the end of that, we thought. However, our paparazzi "pal" had been busy. We were astounded the next day to find ourselves on the front page of every newspaper in Athens.

There we were, a *cause celebre* captured in black and white, with various people putting money in my shoe. A political cartoonist depicted the prime minister of Greece making a contribution.

It seems that a few hippies were beginning to make an incursion into Greece and police thought we might have been part of the vanguard, even though we had short hair.

Almost as an apology to us, a few restaurant owners tracked us down and invited us to come and play for free food. We ate like kings for about three days.

When the gigs and the glory gave out, we gave up "Shoe Business," took our "groupies," and hitchhiked north to Thessalonica, where I waved goodbye to my British chums and headed off alone towards Istanbul and the great beyond.

## Into Asia

In Istanbul I met another Californian, Vernon Tritchka, who was headed to Tehran, Iran. After seeing the Istanbul sights, including the Topkapi museum and the unbelievable Blue Mosque, he and I made our way to Ankara, where he knew Colonel W. P. Sloan, a US Air Force retiree.

I left my American guitar with the colonel, who sold it for me and sent the money to my parents. I kept the old Flamenco guitar, which I had purchased for $40 in Spain. It turned out to be a great traveling companion, opening doors to hearths and homes wherever I went.

Vern and I next boarded a train for Iran, carrying a loaf of bread and jars of jelly and peanut butter, given to us by our American hosts in Ankara. It fed us for two days, as the train wended its way to the end of the line. We next boarded a bus, which was loaded with people, goats, and chickens, and rode the bus as far as it went: a village of mud huts miles away from the Iranian border.

The only transport we could find there was a donkey cart with solid-wood wheels. So, we started walking down a dirt road, only to be stopped by an oncoming station wagon, driven by an American, George Taucher, of Cicero, Illinois, who was working in the area on some government assignment.

He said we were crazy, but when his urging for us to turn back failed, he agreed to turn around and take us to the Iranian border, where we boarded a train bound for Teheran. There I parted company with my peanut-butter-and-jelly pal.


## Mud huts and hit music

I stayed on the train and went with three Peace Corps workers who were en route back to their mud huts in Mashad, near the Afghanistan border. These were three great young men, Pat Sheafor, Jim Kleinbach, and Al Clutter.

Back then, Americans were welcome in Iran, as the United States was an important ally against the Russians. When the Mashad villagers spotted my guitar, they asked me to play at local banquets. These were boisterous affairs with men dancing in circles, leaning over backwards to pick up handkerchiefs off the floor with their teeth.

As a song says, "Those were the days, my friend. I thought they'd never end." However, the party did end, because the food was so abundant I literally got sick of eating and developed gastritis.

When I got ready to head across Afghanistan, my Peace Corps friends discouraged me. "There are three ways to go," they said. "Would you prefer a plague, a tribal war, or landslides?"

I agreed to let them put me on a bus headed south to what was then West Pakistan, known today simply as Pakistan. The bus, filled with people, sheep, and chickens, would periodically stop for bathroom breaks among the sand dunes.

## Roll out the barrel

To fill up the bus gas tank, villagers would roll out a full oil drum, dipping in a measuring stick before and after the fill-up to determine how much was owed for gasoline. While this was happening I wandered down the street and sampled delicacies, such as sheep-eyeball stew.

At one of the stops, a Pakistani man gave me a ride across the desert, cruising past camel caravans in his brand-new '63 Chevrolet, paid for with his earnings in Kuwait. At the Pakistan border, customs guards unrolled the carpet on top of his car and detained him for trying to smuggle in undeclared merchandise. They let me go, stamping a visa in my passport after I paid a generous bribe.

## A whole lot of shaking going on

In Lahore, I was invited to stay a few days at the home of Salim Ahmad and his Pakistani family. They were wonderful hosts, who took me by surprise one morning when they suddenly ran out of the house. There was a low rumbling noise and the house shook.

I ambled outside and found them all squatting in the yard. "Get down! Get down!" they cried, explaining that one can suffer brain damage by standing during an earthquake. (That explains a lot, my wife says.)

## The French connection

When I got to New Delhi I turned around on the street one day and came face to face with a young Frenchman, "Frenchie" Poznanski of Nice, whom I'd met on the freighter out of Barcelona. He said he had been in Afghanistan, doing sketches of ruins, when he came down with some ailment, perhaps malaria. His emaciated appearance made me glad I'd skirted that country!

We teamed up and got a free room in New Delhi's Birla Temple, a place that had been frequented by Gandhi. The temple priests believed in charity for visitors, which included us and lots of monkeys. We slept on wooden frames with rope webbing stretched across them.

We spent our days walking around town in the heat, dodging cows and cow patties, and sweating as fast as we could replace our fluids. I ended up with dysentery. I had already been losing weight, and I soon dropped about ten pounds more. However, when the dysentery stopped, I felt more energy than I've ever felt in my life.

I eventually left Frenchie and headed out of Delhi toward Agra, riding third class on a smoke-belching, steam-powered train. It was so crowded that people were riding in the luggage racks. I wanted to get off and maybe upgrade to second or first class, but that was impossible.

Each time the train stopped more people packed in—people with leprosy, elephantiasis, blindness, and any number of other maladies. It was all I could do to get off when the train got to Agra.

There, I marveled at the majesty of the Taj Mahal. I was captivated by the size of the palace—and amazed at the fine details, such as the translucent finery of the marble carvings. I stood on the rear veranda overlooking a river far below. There were huge yard-long turtles along the bank.

A flurry of large fruit bats fluttered out of the trees as the sun went down. It was magical.


### Dung ho!

A man gave me a place to sleep in a hut just outside the Taj Mahal gate. When I awoke the next morning I started hitchhiking. My first ride was on an ox-drawn cart filled with dried cow dung, which is used for cooking fuel.

I spotted a young girl standing behind a cow, catching the fresh poop before it could hit the ground.

Eventually, I got pooped riding the poop cart, and asked a couple of bearded, turbaned Sikhs to let me ride in the storage box on top of their truck cab. This worked out great for all concerned, since they would ask me to play a song for them every time we stopped.

At one roadside café I went outside to sit on a log to eat my lunch, only to have a hawk swoop down and take off with my food.

Back on the truck, we sped by elephants and monkeys, and I made it safely to Patna.

## An Everest peek

There, I caught a small plane to Katmandu, Nepal. In the air, the pilot suggested we take a look at Mount Everest in the distance. When I landed I later discovered that James Whittaker, the first American to summit the 29,028-foot peak, had made it to the top on the day when I was looking at it.

Nepal was a peak experience for me, too, like going to another planet. I was followed around by scads of children, who thought I was a giant at six feet two inches tall. Although I found the Nepalese to be extremely short, I was amazed at how strong they were, as evidenced by the refrigerator-sized loads some of them managed to carry with the aid of head straps.

One day I went to the top of a small mountain, where Buddha had spent some time. There was a small monastery there, filled with monks in saffron-colored robes, droning on in an other-worldly guttural chant that made the hair on the back of my neck stand up.

## Altitude determines attitude

I met some refugee lamas from Tibet and bought some artifacts from them, including a trumpet, which I later discovered was made from a human leg bone. As I went away from the mountain I passed a parade of musicians following a litter-borne child "god."

In many ways I was on top of the world. I felt totally free. My spirit soared. For nine months I had experienced utter freedom, able to go wherever I pleased. I was halfway around the world from the Mississippi Delta, free of its gravitational force.

Suddenly, it began to feel as though I were floating in space. I had nothing against which to shove off. I was weightless. I decided I should head on home, identifying with the Kris Kristofferson song *Loving Arms,* which says, "I've been too long in the wind, too long in the rain…longing for the freedom of my chains."

The only thing I was sure of was that I wanted to get married and have children.

## Down from the mountain

I headed back to the airport and flew back to Patna, India, to a lower altitude. When we landed, an Indian passenger fainted. One Indian and I were the only ones to rush to his aid. After the fallen passenger was attended by medical authorities, I met my fellow Samaritan.

He invited me to come to his Bengal jungle camp, where he owned a bulldozer and was clearing land. There, he gave me a cot with a mosquito net. I spent a couple of days immersing myself in the local landscape.

When I showered I would go to a well, where a worker would manipulate a boom, which had a huge mud ball on one end and a cloth bag on a rope on the other end. He would lever water out of the well and pour it over me.

Next, I hitchhiked to Calcutta, appropriately named the Black Hole. It was in the grips of a cholera epidemic when I got there. There were occasional dead bodies in the street, awaiting crews to haul them off to feed to vultures or to burn in crematoria. Luckily, I'd had the foresight to get a cholera vaccination in Spain!

I estimate the trip from Athens to Calcutta cost me less than $50, including the $20 round-trip airfare from India to Nepal.

## Out of India

In Calcutta I joined up with a New Zealander and a Brit. We got out of town as quickly as we could, flying to Rangoon, Burma, then Bangkok, Thailand, where we took our stewardess' lodging advice and went to her uncle's "hotel." It turned out to be a hotel-brothel combination, and I must admit that I quite enjoyed the stay. The Thai are a beautiful people.

This is where I got the nightclub job, only to be outdone by a Thai Elvis impersonator, mentioned in Chapter 10.

I later moved to a room in downtown Bangkok, toured all the sights, and flew to Cambodia, where I teamed up with a Scotsman who had just returned from Africa, where he'd served as a soldier, fighting Mau-Mau tribesmen.

## Latter-day Lord Jims

We went to the ruins of Angkor Wat, a vast temple ruin in the jungles. It had been first discovered by Westerners when a French butterfly collector stumbled upon it. It's part of a vast city once populated by the long-gone Khmer civilization.

The temple is surrounded by long moats on each side. We crossed a moat and found a thatched bamboo hut inhabited by Buddhist monks. They offered us a place to sleep, under rows of dried fish hanging from a low ceiling.

We walked around the ruins like two latter-day Lord Jims, buying food from the natives and marveling at the way the tree roots had engulfed some of the old stone structures.

When we got back to our hut, our packs were on the front steps. We missed the subtle hint and went back in to our sleeping quarters. The next day, when we again returned to the hut, our packs were at the end of a path leading away from the hut. We figured we had overstayed our welcome.

## The snakes and arrows of outrageous fortune

That's when we moved into the temple, sleeping on stone floors, with bats flying overhead. One morning I awoke to find a long, green snake stretched out alongside me. I started to get nervous, then saw that he had the tail-half of a large lizard sticking out of his mouth.

I had another scary moment while walking through the jungle. Suddenly a bamboo arrow thwacked into the tree ahead of me. I looked over to see a Cambodian native threading his way through the trees, coming in my direction.

Thank God, he was smiling. I have no idea what he was saying, but he agreed to sell me his crossbow as fast as I could whip a $5 bill out of my pocket. (The crossbow vanished years later in one of my family's cataclysmic yard sales.)

## To Vietnam, where the draft board can't find me

I next went to South Vietnam, where I lived royally for a week on a large wad of Vietnamese piasters, which I had purchased months earlier for $10, a fraction of their value, on the black market in India.

I had shown the wad of money to a number of hotel clerks, who told me it wouldn't last a week, and one of them took pity on me and invited me into his home, where I slept on a bed made of wooden boards.

Consequently, with no room expense, I had enough money to wander around town and eat like a king. One day I had steak-and-lobster dinner for a dollar.

I was blissfully unaware that my hometown draft board was looking for me, so they could try to send me to Vietnam!

When the piasters began to peter out, I decided to splurge on an airline ticket to Hong Kong, where I'd hoped to get a job on a ship to Australia. On my way out of the village where I'd been staying I was pummeled by a throng of little children, who were yelling at me and hitting me with their fists. I just bowed my head and kept walking.

### Viet Cong attack, monk ignites himself

I made it to the airport intact, but my flight was delayed because on that day the Viet Cong made their first raid on the South, attacking the Saigon Airport. My plane left the next day on June 11, 1963, the day a Buddhist monk, Thich Quang Duc, sat calmly in the middle of a Saigon street burning himself to death in protest. People around him were wailing, but he uttered not a word.

His heart, which had not burned, has been enshrined as a sacred relic.

I got out just in time, because it was then that what US politicians were calling a police action began really heating up, eventually becoming an official war.

In Hong Kong I found that the Chinese unions had a lock on most ship jobs, so I decided to fly home, after I finally found a bank that would cash a $200 check from Daddy. I succeeded when a merchant, who was familiar with cotton row in Memphis, agreed to vouch for me. He had no idea who I was, as far as I could tell; or maybe he recognized the Perry name.

### Japan ease

I had a two-week layover in Tokyo, where a Japanese family provided food and lodging in exchange for English lessons for their daughter (who, I'm proud to say, mastered the difference between "l" and "r").

I stayed at the home along with Dr. Walter Wigert, a physician from Barrington, Illinois, who was planning to motorcycle to Europe, across China. I hope he made it.

Tokyo was getting ready to host the Olympics and people often came up to us and asked if they could practice their "Engrish."

### Two birthdays in two days

On July 6, my twenty-second birthday, I crossed the international date line, arriving in Hawaii the day before I left. I was twenty-one again!

I really felt two years older after being invited to stay with and babysit a houseful of kids for a naval officer from Tunica, Mississippi— US Navy Captain Frank Adams, whose claim to fame was being second in command of the Nautilus submarine when it navigated underneath the ice cap at the North Pole. He took me on board a nuclear sub for a tour.

It was at this point that I began to feel like a submariner myself. A slow, sinking feeling set in. Having lost fifty pounds, mostly in India, I was as fit as I've ever been in my life. However, after two weeks of American food, mostly hamburgers, my $10 tailor-made Hong Kong suit began to feel tight.

## The edge of the West Coast

I flew to Seattle, Washington, and visited with Uncle Elmer Whitescarver and his wife, my Aunt Mable, Momma's sister. They were wonderful hosts, as were their sons, Elvin and Billy, and their families.

The airline ticket allowed me to make four stops along the West Coast, but would not allow me to go farther inland. So, I next flew south to Portland, Oregon, then to San Francisco, where I called a fellow I'd met in Greece.

I'd had no idea he was gay, so when he introduced me to his three flamboyant roommates, I made a homophobic call to my old Sacramento buddies, who drove down that day and took me to Sacramento.

We spent a few days reliving our European adventures, until we got thrown out of an apartment building for being too rowdy. We then took our garbage can full of sangria, a wine and fruit concoction, and moved our party to the sidewalk.

When the apartment manager came out with his huge henchmen and tried to evict us from the sidewalk, I backed them all down by striking a karate pose I'd seen in Japan. They bought it, thank God!

We left when we got good and ready, only to be stopped by a cop who never noticed the huge wine container on the car floor. He let us drive on.

Next I flew to California where I visited with Bonehead for a few days before Aunt Ewee put me on a Greyhound bus to Memphis, insisting that it was too dangerous to hitchhike across the US.

### Really, who is this?

When the bus arrived in Memphis, I called home, but it took a few minutes to convince my family it was me. Apparently my voice had dropped a little lower and I had learned to enunciate.

I enjoyed a wonderful homecoming. I was again in orbit around the gravitational field of The Delta.

Soon I was off to Vanderbilt for my senior year. I graduated with a major in English, then attended journalism courses at night school and learned to type.

What followed was a brief journalism career that allowed me to interview a wide range of people, from Loretta Lynn, queen of country music, to Prince Rainier of Monaco.

Georgia & Grandson Jack

Whit, Jack, Rob
Penny

Shiloh

Rob, Adrienne, Whit, Penny, Jack, Amy & Shiloh

# Our Family

# CHAPTER 15

## Full House

---

### I ante a Penny

My carefree bachelor days were finished on August 27, 1966, at age twenty-five, when I married Penelope Wallace Smith, twenty. We've been together for more than forty years.

Penny's maiden name speaks volumes. Smith, derived from *smitar*, "to smite," is very appropriate. I was smitten with her from the start.

I was twenty-four, working as a police reporter for *The Nashville Banner*, a large Tennessee daily newspaper. I knew everyone in and around the police station, getting stories from sources ranging from attorney Fred Thompson, who later became an actor and presidential candidate, to a courthouse regular named Gene Jacobs, known as Little Evil (who got the nickname after he once ran for elected office and was said to be the lesser of two evils).

I even got story ideas from the janitor, a bright, young black man with a PhD, who couldn't find a better job. One day he introduced me to Penny, a nineteen-year-old college student who was working as a summer aide to the police chief, a job she had obtained by working in someone's political campaign. "She likes to write, too," my janitor friend said. "She writes poetry."

Penny usually tells people we were introduced by the vice squad, which makes a better story. A vice-squad detective did lead to our first date, though, when he mentioned he had found a moonshine still in a remote cave near the cabin where I was living.

### Moonshine magic

The cabin was in the woods, partially cantilevered over a cliff about one hundred feet above the Stone's River, which was soon to be dammed to form a lake.

Vandals had been breaking into the house and the owner, a prominent Nashville attorney, had let me live there for free, to protect his vacation house while he fought with the federal government in a futile attempt to keep them from taking it.

Years later I returned to the site, which now overlooks Percy Priest Lake. There's a restroom building there now, a far cry from the romantic spot where Penny and I had our first date after exploring the cave.

To find the cave, we had walked through the woods. We were exuberant and even climbed a tree before plunging into the cavern, where we sat in the dark and kissed.

## Deep in love

When I turned on my flashlight in the cave, I realized we had been sitting on a pile of bat guano. You might say I was *in deep*, in more ways than one.

At the cabin, we grilled steaks, had a few drinks, and sat on the porch.

Below, on the other side of the river, flat farmland stretched out under a full moon. A dog howled in the distance. The river rippled past. It was a magical evening.

We had another magical evening two weeks later, a date that was marred by the fact that the dishes from the first date were still piled up in the kitchen sink. She knew then that I needed domesticating. We had been mixed irretrievably together in the "Cosmic Cuisinart," as one *Newsweek* writer labeled couples' karma.

## Moving to Memphis

I moved to Memphis to work as a columnist and reporter for *The Commercial Appeal*, and we dated on and off while Penny attended the University of Tennessee in Knoxville. One of my letters, written after she visited me for four days, tells of an "all-encompassing ache" which I felt after she left.

I waxed as eloquent as I could: "That ache stems from an ever-increasing dependence on you. That dependence is the price one must pay to really LOVE someone. And that price, in this case, is the biggest bargain in town.

"Imagine, just when you're on top of the world you suddenly come across an endless ladder, spiraling to new, dizzying heights. You are my opium, Nirvana, my other half."

She said she was floating across the UT campus as she read that, only to be brought back down to earth, somewhat, by my parting line: "And if all that crap ain't gettin' through to ya' Baby, you're still the greatest."

The next summer she moved to Memphis, after I talked her out of a summer job in the Catskills. It was all over.

## Weave got it good

Penelope, which is Greek for "weaver," had woven herself permanently into the fabric of my life.

She proved a good sport when I took her to visit in Mississippi, once faithfully carrying a baby-food jar on a coon hunt, after Daddy had convinced her that coons, like 'possums, have babies small enough for a litter to fit into a small "coon jar."

Every time we shot a coon, Penny would run up with the open baby-food jar. "Never mind," my brothers would say with mock disappointment, "it's another male coon."

Penny also was gullible enough to marry me, and she stood by me years later when I underwent a spinal fusion, which crippled me for about six months and has plagued me ever since. In spite of my weak back and poor health, she insisted that we not delay plans to have children. We had two sons. It's the best decision we've ever made.

## The prince and the pauper

Before I tell you about my sons, let me tell you about another man besides Daddy who had a profound effect on me.

I was on the trail of Prince Rainier of Monaco in the mid-1960s when I first met Kemmons Wilson, the Holiday Inns founder who died in 2003, at age ninety.

I was a brash young Memphis newspaper reporter, attempting to crash a small, private reception for the prince, a potential Holiday Inn franchisee.

My editor at *The Commercial Appeal* had asked me to do whatever I had to do to get the interview.

It was easy, once I discovered where the prince was, because Kemmons Wilson treated *me* like royalty.

"Come on in," he said, flashing his boyish grin and promptly escorting me to the prince. After a brief interview, I went to phone it in. To my surprise, I was invited to return to the party to visit some more with the prince.

## I get to know the *real* prince

More importantly, I got to know Kemmons, who as a child in Arkansas was paupered when his father died. Although he never graduated from high school, he had created and now ruled a vast hotel/motel empire.

About a year later I was invited to head up the Holiday Inns public relations department. The company was on a quest to be a worldwide contender—and the fact that I'd traveled around the world appealed to them. I leapt at the opportunity and had a great five-year career there.

One of my favorite responsibilities was helping Kemmons with speeches, often flying around the country with him on the corporate Lear jet, soaking up his down-home wisdom.

## A *TIME*-ly query

In 1972 I wrote the editor of *TIME* magazine, loading him down with information that I felt merited a major story. By this time there were

1,480 Holiday Inns in twenty-three countries and territories, with new inns under construction on every continent except Antarctica.

To my delight, *TIME* followed up by sending a reporter and famed photojournalist Alfred Eisenstaedt, a diminutive man whose giant career, by then, included almost one hundred *Life* magazine cover shots.

A few months later more than six million *TIME* covers flashed Kemmons' smiling face and the Holiday Inn sign around the world, under the banner, "The Man With 300,000 Beds."

The cover story related Kemmons' Horatio Alger story: "Like many visionaries, he takes an uncomplicated view of the world that leaves little room for doubt. 'When you've got an idea,' he says, 'you've got to think of a reason for doing it, not of a reason for not doing it.'"

## Nuggets of wisdom

Here are seven nuggets of wisdom from Kemmons:

1.  **Don't orate**. Kemmons could give a rousing commencement speech in a couple of minutes. He knew most audiences didn't want to hear someone droning on and on. Speaking as incoming president of the National Heart Fund in Dallas, he tossed aside my suggested speech and, instead, simply told a joke I'd shared with him on the plane. This was basically his entire speech: "I used to smoke, until one day my son asked me what I was doing. I said, 'I'm smoking.' My son looked up at me and replied, 'No you're not! The cigarette is smoking. You're just the sucker!'" He got a standing ovation and sat down.

2.  **Work hard**. "Only work half a day. It doesn't matter which half you work, the first twelve hours or the second twelve hours… I start early and stay at it late, six days a week. When we are actively working towards a goal, the hours pass quickly. Work is not a man's doom but rather his blessing."

3.  **Control your time**. When traveling, Kemmons would save time by ordering dessert first, then eating it while his meal was being prepared. On plane trips he would dictate

correspondence. A remarkable letter was shared with me by his secretary. On the tape, Kemmons was in the middle of a letter, paused, then commented matter-of-factly, "The engine's on fire," before resuming dictation as the plane crash-landed. I guess it had helped that he had flown supply runs over the Himalayas in World War II. He emerged with only bruises, but one passenger died.

4. **Be honest**. Kemmons believed in doing business with a handshake, which drove the corporate attorneys nuts. On his office wall was a framed quotation from Shakespeare's *Henry VI:* "The first thing we do is kill all the lawyers."

5. **Stay curious**. His desk was always cluttered, reflecting a mind that was curious about virtually everything. "If a cluttered desk is a sign of a cluttered mind," he told me, "then what does an empty desk mean?"

6. **Work for yourself**. "The last time I worked for someone else was doing bookkeeping," he told me. "There was an older man there who died and they promoted me to his job, but they didn't give me his pay. I quit."

7. **Don't be afraid of failure**. "I don't want to succeed at everything," he said. "I just want to be right more than half the time." In his first successful business venture he owned a popcorn machine on wheels, which he operated in the lobby of a Memphis movie theater—until the theater manager determined that Kemmons was making more money than the theater. He eventually got into real estate and had some notable failures, once building a house on the wrong lot. He built an ice-skating rink, which he eventually covered with dirt, making it into a rodeo arena. He briefly owned an Orange Crush bottling plant, until he realized even his own kids hated the drink. He turned down Sun Records' offer to sell him Elvis Presley's contract for a pittance.

In the June 12, 1972, cover story, *TIME* called him a "bluff, zesty man who believes absolutely in the company motto that is imprinted on the necktie that he wears: 'It's a wonderful world'" (pp. 77-82).

If there ever were a pauper turned into a prince, it was Kemmons

Wilson, kissed by fate and blessed with a burning desire to leave his footprints in the sands of time. Who else but a prince could sidle up to the king of Morocco, put his arm around him, and say, simply, "Hey King!"—and then start looking for somewhere to build?

## We build a family

I felt like a king when our two sons were born, but when our first son, Jack Whitley Perry II, was three, Penny and I were brought to our knees when he developed diabetes. We virtually became his primary-care physicians for the next nine years, until he was able to begin to manage the disease himself.

Thinking I would have more time at home to help with Jack, I left my job at Holiday Inns International and moved to Georgia to head up the marketing department of Callaway Gardens, a large horticultural and recreational resort near Pine Mountain.

I had less time at home! So, I took Kemmons' advice and went into business for myself, first as a freelance writer and then as a financial planner.

When Jack would have seizures from insulin shock, our younger son, Rob, would stand and watch as we force-fed Jack with orange juice and crackers, frantically trying to raise his blood sugar level and bring him back into a state of coherence.

One time Rob asked, "When am I going to get my diabetes?" That was heartbreaking. Luckily he made it into his thirties before the genetic disease caught up to him.

## So far, so good

Both sons are doing extremely well and we could not be prouder. When we moved to Georgia, Penny became a brilliant teacher of gifted children. Parents and former students often stop me on the street to brag about what a great teacher she was. One parent called her a "treasure."

However, she later had to retire early and draw a disability pension.

In Greek mythology there is a woman named Penelope who says she will keep her promise when she completes the tapestry she is weaving. Each night, she unravels the previous day's work.

As we go into the last chapter of our lives, we still work on the tapestry, weaving it back together each time it unravels.

We are rich, according to this Native American proverb: "The soul would have no rainbow if the eye had no tear."

## We try farm life

One of the most interesting phases of our family life was in the 1970s, when I was trying my hand at full-time writing and we had moved a double-wide trailer onto an abandoned farm three miles up a primitive dirt road outside LaGrange.

My friends, Bill and Ann Petry, owned the land and were attempting to recover some of the property from the forest, including an old kudzu-covered farmhouse, which had nearly collapsed. It was located in the middle of nowhere, several miles from other homes, except for a widow who lived about a half mile away with her grown sons.

Each weekday Penny carted our two boys to grammar school, leaving me alone in the middle of nowhere with a typewriter and our faithful dog, Bingo, a German shepherd mix that had appeared mysteriously at our door.

"Daddy, there's a skunk under the porch," the kids had yelled. It was a puppy, so mangy that it looked two-toned. We nursed it back to health, lacing its food with lard until it became a truly handsome dog.

I took to rambling in the woods with Bingo whenever writer's block struck, which was quite often.

## Strange happenings

Weird things would happen. The most unnerving thing at first was the total absence of man-made noises. This didn't last too long, because one day I got knocked flat by a roar that shook the forest. Some fighter pilot periodically loved to streak over the treetops in his jet, so fast and so low that he was long gone before I could hear him coming.

On other days the thunder came from a herd of wild cows that swept through the brush like stampeding bison.

I heard that the cows were owned by an elderly LaGrange man, and if you killed one, he would demand repayment—unless it ran out of the woods and crashed into your car, in which case he would claim, "That cow definitely was not mine!"

Allegedly, the herd evolved from his practice of loaning people pregnant cows; you got some milk and you also got to raise a calf for him.

What I do know for sure was that, when I finally got a garden ready for harvest, something pillaged the whole plot, leaving nothing but cow tracks. I telephoned the cows' "owner."

Then in his nineties, he arrived at the crime scene in his chauffeur-driven pickup. I asked him, in my most forceful Southern dialect, "What you gon' *do* 'bout it?" He offered no restitution.

I hinted that my shotgun might soon provide him with "the first herd shot around the world." He left and the cows soon disappeared. Some say his son rounded them up and sold them.


## The wild dog invasion

Regardless, peace returned to the woods—until the wild dogs came.

There were three of them. They'd slink up and persuade Bingo to desert us for days at a time. He'd always return, haggard and bloodied.

Realizing it was time to *do* something, I resolved the problem with three loads of buckshot. After my three-dog night, I got a call from the widow's family announcing that they'd found a wounded dog. That's how we acquired Brownie, one of the dogs I'd shot. We took her in and nursed her back to health, and what a wonderful addition to the family she was.

Enter Hogzilla Jr.—a smaller version of Hogzilla, the huge wild boar that later made headlines elsewhere in Georgia.

For months I'd been noticing that some mysterious feral hog was plowing ruts throughout the vast woods surrounding us. Then, one night Bingo and Brownie went nuts. Armed with shotgun and flashlight, I waded into the night and came upon a blur of dogs swirling around a huge hog.

I pumped three loads of buckshot into the beast and it just stood there, implacable. I fired a slug and that seemed to motivate him to move on. When he got to the road, he dropped.

## Oops!

I called the widow's sons, explaining that I'd killed a wild hog that they might enjoy eating. Soon I heard a car on the road, followed by the sound of slamming doors as the car left.

Soon the phone rang: "You done shot our hog!"

I explained that I was deeply sorry, but that the hog obviously had been running wild for months.

"What you gon' do 'bout it?" they asked.

"Well, if you don't want the meat I'll borrow a tractor and drag it into the woods tomorrow."

"Naw," said the voice. "I mean what you gon' *do* 'bout it?"

I explained I wasn't *gon' do* anything. When they threatened to call the sheriff I offered to give them the telephone number.

The hog carcass was donated to the buzzards and that was the last I heard on the subject, until the first cold day of fall. The phone rang. It was the widow's family: "Will you come up here and shoot our hogs?"

I obliged and that was the last time I fired a gun. We later moved into town and I sold my shotgun and rifles.

## How a grandchild can clear a cloudy future

My only hope for genetic immortality rests on the wee, unsuspecting shoulders of one little girl—my granddaughter, Shiloh Bay Perry.

Her name struck me as unusual at first, but now that it is so totally inhabited by her it has become some sort of celestial music to my ears.

And, although it sounds like Shallow Bay, it certainly belies the depth of my gene pool.

Lacking quantity, this pool is teeming with quality; at least that's the way I see it. If Family Fate produces no more grandchildren, I cannot imagine a better draw of the karmic cards than Shiloh.

Now that I'm plumb giddy with grandpa-itis, I'm sure a lot of grandparents know the feeling, in spades—which puts me to wondering, "Where does this come from?"

It has got to be more than an extension of the inherent biological imperative to go and be fruitful. Is it our way of leaving more than our footprints in the sands of time?

## Immortality and immorality

Throughout history people have tried their hands at immortality, most notably the Egyptians. The notion of immortality is as old as the notion of immorality; just as there was original sin, there was an original sense of something more to life than life itself.

I believe that the Egyptian pharaohs were just the best of many self-centered dynastic dingbats who felt they could fill up an immobile U-Haul with earthly goodies (even pets and servants) and hook it all to some sort of celestial hearse bound for eternity.

If they had been really smart, they would've asked the embalmers to leave in those "minor" organs, such as hearts and brains. (It's scary to think that if they were right there's going to be a Pharaoh Section of eternity filled with a heartless horde of mindless mummies.)

Much more appealing, and accessible to all classes of mankind, is the religious concept of a limitless spiritual continuum—the eternal better place we usually refer to, especially when a loved one dies in severe pain.

Meanwhile, back here on earth, there is the inexplicable hope that we find in the children. As John Denver once sang, "Their laughter and their loveliness can clear a cloudy day."

Like an antidote to aging, grandchildren give us hope in the face of an inevitable departure. It's the old notion that "when one door closes, another door opens."

And, boy, did my younger brother, George, blow that door open! His five children have given him fourteen grandchildren—and still counting. George is a farmer through and through, and he revels in his crop of descendants like he'd won every blue ribbon at a 4-H competition.

## Going deep

His greatest hobby now is tracking down his family tree. I guess when he saw so much possibility for the future, he suddenly had to counterbalance it by looking back. Now he's plowing so deeply through family roots we're expecting him to pop up in China any day.

It does my heart good, because I was the one always interested in the family stories; not the dates, and the who-begat-who details, but the why and the how. I was the one who drifted away from my siblings to eat a cathead biscuit and soak up stories at Grandmomma's house. I would sit for hours, eagerly listening to Miss Sallie's tales of the good old days.

My grandparents and my parents still exist in Living Memory. In this book I'm striving to write down all the good stuff (before I lose the key to my mental filing system, or worse). Why would I do that? For Shiloh, of course. They never knew her, but she can know them.

As William Faulkner wrote, "The past is not dead. In fact, it's not even past."

## Coming up roses

And Shiloh can know details about the day she was born one late September when our son, Jack, summoned us to the Columbus, Georgia, hospital where his wife, Amy, was in labor.

After Shiloh had successfully made her entrance into this world, Penny and I returned home, tired and full of joy. Then Penny noticed the rosebush that she had planted in her English garden just months earlier.

The planting instructions said the bush would produce no blooms until the second year. But there it was, among the thorns: one perfect rose bloom, pristinely, proudly, and prematurely right on time.

## Memories

I can identify with Larry McMurtry's *Lonesome Dove* character, Gus McCrae, who said: "I gave life a good go."

Just how good it has been is reflected in some of the mementos from our sons.

Rob, the son who's taller than I, once gave me a plaque that I treasure. It says, "A father is someone you look up to, no matter how tall you are."

The first time he went off to summer camp Penny and I wanted to stretch his umbilical cord through the postal system, so we sent him off with a large supply of stamped, self-addressed envelopes. Just to be safe, Penny also threw in a handful of 3 x 5 cards, each with its own instructions: "Check one: 'I'm great,' 'I'm unhappy,' or 'I'm okay.'"

One of the return cards is stashed away in our memory drawer. In the "I'm okay" box is a blob of ink, which must have drained half his ballpoint pen. On the back is this epistle: "Dear mom and dab I stong by a wast or it was a horsafly in the middle of my eyes. I have five feinds."

There is also a sentence completion questionnaire, a grammar school exercise in which Rob had to finish various sentences. Some examples:

*Mothers don't*: "twirl their kids on their fingers."

*I can never*: "eat the whole earth."

Rob had a good sense of humor, but he was serious when it came to regular homework. He got several college scholarships and opted to work every other quarter in the Georgia Tech co-op program, graduating with highest honors, lots of job experience, and money in the bank.

Also in the memory drawer are his 3 x 5 cards outlining his high-school salutatorian speech. As I'm reading his speech I'm looking for drops of sweat on the cards, because of the agony he went through.

The speech opener was: "My job tonight is to speak for a few minutes. Your job is to listen for a few minutes. I hope you don't finish before I do." He closed with: "As you slide down the banister of Time, may all the splinters point in the right direction."

May they indeed, Rob!

Rob is now an engineer with Ford Motor Company, working in Louisville, Kentucky. His wife, Adrienne, is a former engineer from LaGrange (Kentucky, not Georgia), and is now a CPA, also working for Ford.


## Our jumping Jack

There are mementos, too, from Jack, my rambunctious son. The one I like best is the paperweight he made for me, a flat rock, eight inches long, the shape of the state of Virginia, painted green, with an eye and a row of teeth drawn to resemble an alligator head. On the bottom is pasted a piece of paper that says: "To Dad on his 30 no 40th birthday. Love, Jack."

Jack was eleven when he found the rock, on a hike at a camp for kids with diabetes near Waco, Georgia. The stone apparently screamed at him from the forest floor: "Help! I'm an alligator head! Take me home and paint me green and give me to your dad on his 30 no 40th birthday. And, oh yes, it would be great to use the hood of your dad's car to paint me." (Luckily, I had a green car.)

Today I smile every time the alligator sticks his head out of the murky clutter of my desk.

I smile at the dueling Mother's Day cards. The one from Rob says, "My little hands, Dear Mother, are not very strong, but I'll show you how much I love you by being helpful all day long."

Not to be outdone, Jack wrote a card saying, "My hands are *storng* but they can be gentle and they can love you very much."

Jack is a computer programmer in Columbus, Georgia, working with TSYS, one of the world's largest processors of credit cards. His wife, Amy, is a technical writer with the same company.

They live just a half hour from us in a beautiful house overlooking a creek with about ten little waterfalls. They enjoy Shiloh and we get to see her often.

Jack will have to write his life story for Shiloh some day, adding an end to the Jack saga, unless Shiloh has a son and names him Jack. Maybe, if they'll let me in the Jack Club (as "J, the quarter Jack") he can add his chapter and reissue this book as *3.25 Jacks.*

# IT'S ALL RELATIVE

*Miss Sallie's great-great grandfather, Captain Jack Taylor*

*My link to a cornucopia of new cousins, "The Taylors of Tabernacle"*

*Calling all cousins*

*Harold Taylor, Tina Gray, Rod Taylor*

*The Edwin Speed Taylor Camp*

*Richard Taylor, his ancestor by the same name and the original house*

*The 1826 Corn Crib*

# CHAPTER 16

## Royal Flush

### Royal flesh

There's a memorable bit of movie dialog in the *Butch Cassidy and the Sundance Kid* movie, when Butch assures Sundance that the trackers dogging them "can't track us over rocks."

"Tell them that," Sundance says, referring to the pursuing posse picking its way along the outlaws' trail.

Butch looks back, then asks, "Who *are* those guys?"

This is what I asked myself when I set out to write about who my father and my grandfather were. I had no idea that I would actually be able to trace my ancestry all the way back to a passel of English and European kings—and *even* Noah and Adam, all joking aside (read on and I'll show you how).

My brother George, now that he has fourteen grandchildren, had already worked up a family tree with all the names and dates, going back a few hundred years. Frankly, this bored the heck out of me.

Like Butch Cassidy, I had to ask: "But *who* were these guys?" So, I set out to put some meat on the bones, starting with the stuff that I knew, and working back from that. I had no real interest in going back further than my grandparents until I got invited to go on a genealogical tour of Mason, in West Tennessee, led by my newly discovered genealogist cousin, John Marshall.

I met some more new cousins on the trip and it seemed that all of us soon caught the genealogy bug.

One cousin, Robyn Whitley Dowdall of Atlanta, even wrote several poems about the experience, including one that starts out like this:

*We stood in the shadow of the great oak tree, some of us strangers until that day. But our loved ones' spirits united us all in a mysterious eternal way.*

*We walked in awe where they walked. We walked where they danced and prayed. And drawing near to the great oak tree, we lifted this thought in prayer:*

*"Tell us God, by your Grace, do they really know we're here?"*

Being a wise guy, I had to ask Robyn, "Do they know that I'm not *all there?*"

(Robyn is a granddaughter of Howard Whitley, who was taken in and reared by his sister, Miss Sallie, when he was an infant. When Howard was grown he was offered a "child's share" of my grandparents' estate if he would stay on the farm. However, he fell in love and married a sixteen-year-old girl who wanted no part of it. Love won out and Howard forsook a potentially big inheritance.)

### Dancers and prayers

On our Mason tour, John Marshall told us that Miss Sallie's mother, Mary Taylor "Totsie" Somervell Whitley, was a member of the Dancing Taylors and that her family was kin to another group known as the Praying Taylors.

He explained that the Taylors were among the first families who migrated to the area, coming from Mecklenburg County, Virginia, and that some were Methodist (praying) and others (my forebears) were Episcopalian and not opposed to men and women dancing together at parties.

For example, after a wedding it was common for the bride's family to have a dining—what we would call a dinner party. The next night there might be another dining at the groom's family home. At these parties some attendees would begin to dance to fiddle tunes and others would go off into other rooms to show their disapproval, presumably to pray for the dancing sinners.

## It's a small world

When I got home to LaGrange, Georgia, I called my good friend, Harold Taylor, and asked him where in Tennessee his family has its annual camp meeting. He and I attend the same church and meet for lunch occasionally. I recalled his mentioning a big and wonderful family reunion. "It's near Brownsville," Harold said.

This is just a few miles from Mason, my grandparents' old stomping grounds, and it turns out Harold's a cousin! However, it seemed he's on the praying side and I'm on the dancing side. (He can pray better than I can dance, that's for sure.)

In July of 2008 Harold invited me to tag along with him to the 182nd "Taylors of Tabernacle" camp meeting, a weeklong affair held in a cluster of forty-two rustic cabins at Tabernacle Methodist Church, near Brownsville, Tennessee. It could be the nation's longest-running family reunion/camp meeting—a holdover of the prolonged brush-arbor revivals that were popular in the early 1800s.

The meeting was the subject of a 1982 feature article in *TIME* magazine, which said, "The kinfolks' reunion and camp meeting have been the beginning and end of the Taylor's year...for eight generations. They come from all over North America, many now called Claiborne or Thornton or one of a dozen other surnames..."

All of the cabins are owned by descendants of Howell Taylor, who shared a grandfather with at least two of my ancestors. This made me a double cousin to the Tabernacle camp crews, a fact that was not lost on me when I was speedily welcomed like a lost sheep into the Edwin Speed Taylor camp.

## All the man's kings

"Here's that Dancing Taylor," proclaimed Tina Gray, as she hugged me alongside the twenty-foot-long dining table which was laden with all kinds of goodies, from fried chicken to chocolate pie.

My new cousin Tina is a genealogy researcher with the Elma Ross Public Library in Brownsville, and shared with me that I may be descended from kin of Presidents George Washington, James Madison, and Zachary Taylor.

She said my lineage also includes the kings of England, plus the medieval European king, Charlemagne (Charles the Great), regarded today as the father of Europe because his empire, in the 700s A.D. and early 800s, united most of Western Europe for the first time since the Romans.

She later sent me charts that took my lineage of English royalty back to such famous names as Henry VIII and Edward I (Longshanks, who was challenged by William Wallace). I pored over the charts until I got a brain cramp.

The list went on and on back to Athelwulf, and his father, Ecgberht, whose reigns were in the 800s A.D. Also included was literature that states that Athelwulf could trace his lineage back for many generations to Cerdic, the fifth-century founder of Wessex, a kingdom in what later would become southern England.

Some scholars allege that Cerdic was not only the forebear of the modern kings of England, but had roots going back to virtually every royal family in Europe.

## Competitive ancestry

It is said that after the ancient Scottish kings claimed that their own ancestry went back to Greek kings and Egyptian pharaohs, the Kings of Wessex got busy with their own family trees, not wanting to be outdone. In 854 they produced documents going back from Ecgberht to a lengthy succession of names, from Ealmund, Eafa, Eoppa, and so on for more than thirty names, all the way back to Sceaf ("That is, the son of Noah, who was born in Noah's ark") and then on back, name by name, to Enos, Seth, and "Adam the first man, and our Father, that is, Christ. Amen."

So there! That's my story and I'm sticking to it! Take that, you Scots newcomers!

Now, let's all join hands and sing, "We are the world, we are the children..."

For now, I'm just going to have to take Tina's word on all these new connections. What I am sure of is that it won't get me a discount at Starbucks.

Even if Tina is wrong, John Marshall says that another cousin had our lineage traced from my great-great-great-great-grandmother, Mary Goodloe Somervell, back to Alfred the Great. "The irony," he said, "is that practically everybody is descended from royalty from centuries ago; it's just a matter of finding your line."

So a royal flush is what happens to your sense of importance when you start thinking you're something special.


## The lost sheep

All this uppity ancestry aside, I'm genuinely excited about finding my huge new Taylor "family" and being treated royally at their kinfolks camp meeting. I felt somewhat like the itinerate preacher, Freeborn Garrettson, who visited with the early American Taylors in 1777. He wrote that he was treated "more like a son than a stranger; yea, I may say, more like an angel than a poor clod of earth."

One morning at the "Love Feast" meeting at the Tabernacle Methodist Church, a service where people stand up and share the good news in their lives, I was introduced by Harold as a "miracle." He explained that we had known each other for fifteen years without knowing that we were, miraculously, related. "I knew there was some reason I liked him," he said.

I stood up and explained about the Dancing Taylors, mock-warning the congregation that some of the Praying Taylors had come dangerously close to "crossing over" to my group when they started leaning from side to side while singing the hymn, *Leaning on Jesus,* from old Cokesbury Worship Hymnals. We had a good laugh.

Back at the camp cabin, our group was regaled by tales of family lore. Harold and his brilliant brother, Rod, also waxed eloquent on Einstein-level theories. It was a stimulating way to while away the time.

Other meetings involved the blessing and baptism of new members, a memorial service for the departed, and a Heritage Walk at the adjoining Taylor cemetery, where Susan Thornton led different participants in reading aloud sections of the three-volume family history, *The Taylors of Tabernacle.*

## Olden days

Leafing through the old Taylor books gives me a better understanding of what my forebears went through. It goes back to my ancestor James Taylor, a schoolteacher and surveyor, whose three sons emigrated from England to America. Our ancestor was James' son, John Taylor, born in the 1600s.

John was grandfather to Howell Taylor, patriarch of the Praying Taylors, to whom all the kinfolk trace their lineage. These early Taylors were "men of the highest order of piety," according to an 1862 issue of the *Western Methodist Advocate*.

"Father Howell was a patriarch, bald as Elisha and venerable as he was bald and aged," it states. "His eccentricities were all innocent, and as he enjoyed them, no one objected to them. He was plain, candid and outspoken."

He had a horror of all secret associations, including Masons, the account states, indicating his belief in the notion that, "Men love darkness rather than light, because their deeds are evil."

It further says that, to this Taylor, "Everything was made subservient to religion. If anything was to be neglected, it was not the cause of God."

Not everyone was as religious back then, and some men of the time were said to be "wild as boars." There was a fear that some might go off the deep end and leave their farms to "tottering old men and green unpracticed boys."

It cites the case of a Mrs. Jones, who disobeyed her husband's orders to refrain from going to hear a Methodist preacher. Mr. Jones became enraged and swore he "would charge his gun and shoot her when she returned."

On her return, the woman "accosted him mildly, and said, 'My dear, if you take my life you must obtain leave of my heavenly Spouse,' and, thus saying, approached him and took the deadly weapon out of his hand without meeting any resistance." The man would later become a Methodist.

The Taylors' Methodism was powerful. Cousin John Marshall reports that in researching one of his books on the history of Mason, he found that one of the visitors to a similar camp meeting reported he had "gotten religion for the eighth time," having gotten it "better than ever before."

In the early 1800s the Taylors made their way from Mecklenburg County, Virginia, to western Tennessee, settling around Brownsville, in Haywood County, about 1826.

The oldest remaining structure at the present campground site is the 1826 corncrib, where an early Taylor family had to sleep on occasion, stating "No one felt the least grieved with rough fair and humble doings."

And rough it was. An old account tells of horses being killed by buffalo gnats and of hunters killing twenty bears one year (it then laments the fact that bear meat was getting scarce the next year).

Next to the crib is the early home of Howell's son, Richard. Surrounded by descendants of early asparagus plants and scuppernong vines, it is being lovingly restored by Richard's descendant, also Richard Taylor, who gave me a tour, pointing out the original stair rails and intact poplar floors.

"The house told me its story as I took it apart," Richard said.

There is another story told in camp that Richard's wife insisted they move in with their three sons while the restoration was in progress. The story alleges that, when told that the bathroom and kitchen were not yet completed, the wife opted for completing the bathroom first, stating that she didn't need a kitchen.

*These* Taylors are still pioneering!

## Longing and belonging

When I left the camp meeting it was with a sense of longing and belonging. On the last morning of my visit I got up at sunrise and took my guitar to the obelisk tombstone of Howell Taylor. I began strumming softly enough to keep from waking the living (and the dead) and quietly began singing *Early Mornin'*, an old Kingston Trio song (by Randy Starr and Dick Wolf):

*It was early in the day when I set out to roam.*
*Went to seek my fortune far away from home...*

I was haunted by the pioneer spirit that propelled my forebears to strike out into this part of the world. Howell Taylor wrote to his son Edmund, "I never was better pleased with any country than this," citing the rich land ("cheap, from two to four dollars per acre") and the flowing springs. But his sights were on another place: "Oh let us struggle on, my son," he wrote, "until we gain the price where pleasure never dies."

## The richness of life

And what a struggle it was. Just a few of the opportunities, challenges and problems, picked randomly from the Taylor diaries, give you an idea of the richness of life back then:

"Warping cloth…making a fish trap…hauling a wagonload of cotton…attending a temperance meeting…making bricks…working on a cabin…tin peddler here today…got 1,000 pounds of pork for $25…rolling logs…battalion muster…cutting a road…visit to tan yard…lent Brother Jones my mare to ride the circuit on…sent wheat to mill…cut a coon tree and got one…kiln-drying planks…clock peddler here…went to settle some difficulty among the negroes… hauling oats…swapped my riding mare for a piece of land…saw the moon hanging on the point…the cholera is in Memphis…grass likely to devour my crops…had tooth pulled…smallpox in Trenton… vaccinated negroes…killed hogs…had a son this morning which died…pulled 3,000 pounds of cotton today…thought there would be a division in the M. E. Church upon the subject of slavery… grandfather died in his 91st year; sleep on aged Pilgrim…never saw so dry a time…making negro shoes…cotton crowded with lice…partridge hunting…made me a sleigh…killed a fawn…sold my cotton and knocked around town [Memphis]…looked for lost saddlebag…looking for ox but found him not…miserable life is mine with no companion but the crickets and my own pen…ran a deer 25 miles; shot him 7 times and then did not kill him…how strange that woman is nothing but a solid mass of fickleness…hare hunt with 30 hounds…took a dose of laudanum and a good dose of mercury…an awful cloud hove in sight; one third of the trees on my farm nearly are down…got some gunpowder and busted an old tree open and fooled the whole country, making them believe that a boat was coming."

My favorite entry for being over the top is: "The ladies made their appearance at the breakfast table arrayed in all the purity and innocence of their own loveliness and as I would throw a glance around upon their lovely erect forms and beautiful figures and countenances beaming with purity the ravages of Cupid were praying upon my inmost soul until I became perfectly lost in the whirl pool stratagena."

Much more down-to-earth is this year-end musing, written in 1846: "The year has been gentle in its move—seed time and harvest each in their turn have kept the rounds to which they have been accustomed for thousands of years."

## A grave meditation

I like what was written about Edmund Taylor in the 1867 *Western Methodist Advocate*:

"Old age has not made him fretful nor peevish. He is a noble example of the power of our holy religion to give cheerfulness to age, and to bless it with wit that is harmless, mirth that is innocent, friendship that is firm, and peace that is undying.

"He lingers like the sun, on the verge of the horizon, tingeing the far off clouds with rosy hues."

Sitting there in the graveyard, alone, as the rosy hues of dawn slanted in among the gravestones and trees, I was in awe of the religious spirit and the family unity that still exists among my new Taylor family. I thought about a 1989 poster, done by someone named Matilda, on the wall of the Edwin Speed Taylor camp.

It says, "The only thing we can take from this life is our family."

It makes my old heart dance!

# LOOK HOMEWARD ANGEL

The Whitley Graves

*This poignantly beautiful statue, with a downcast visage, stands vigil over the graveyard at Old Trinity Church near Mason, Tennessee, where my Whitley grandparents are buried.*

# CHAPTER 17

## Folding

### Going home

Sometimes I rummage through reminders of my youthful around-the-world odyssey, which include a weathered passport (with extra pages glued in for the many visas) and a few grainy photos.

There's also a beat-up little address book, which I lost somewhere along the way. It was found and mailed to me by a kind California gentleman, Gerald Bliss. I like to look through it, finding names of long-forgotten contacts such as "Most Noble P. Suduna, Baron of Tabman."

What I treasure most are Buddhist artifacts that I bought from refugee monks who had escaped from Tibet into Nepal. They include a jeweled money purse and a flint carrier for making fires.

Two of the mementoes deal with death—a wood and leather *damaru*, or prayer drum (usually made with two human skulls), and a *kangling* trumpet, carved from a human thigh bone, perhaps from a virgin.

According to Peter Matthiessen in his classic book *The Snow Leopard* (New York: The Viking Press, 1978), these instruments are "...used in Tantrism to deepen meditation, not through the encouragement of morbid thoughts but as a reminder that our time on earth is fleeting" (p. 211).

If I were to blow on the horn and thump the drum, I would recognize the sound. It is, in the words of Bob Seger, autumn closing in. Some day, gravity *will* win. And I'll be deep *in* The Delta again.

We take the days or years that God gives us and eventually the light of life fades and goes dim, turning inevitably to darkness, the default mode of the universe. How will those of the future know we were here, that we laughed and loved and had our time in the sun?

William Faulkner (*Faulkner in the University, Session 8*, 1959) offers the solution: "Really the writer doesn't want success… He knows he has a short span of life, that the day will come when he must pass through the wall of oblivion, and he wants to leave a scratch on that wall—Kilroy was here—that somebody a hundred, or a thousand years later will see."

My message is simply this: We were here, *every one of us*—or, as they used to say in old English, *every man jack!*

# EPILOGUE

## Paean to a peon

Cousin Robyn Whitley Dowdall surprised me by penning the following poem. In jest, I called it a "paean to a peon," feeling unworthy. I must admit I feel honored.

### *A Young Man's Journey*

He departed the blackened Delta earth
   the fertile land of his Father

He longed to view other worlds
   far from the yielding sod of his youth

His young man's spirit yearned to touch
   other souls, other creeds

He set forth with uncertain courage
   girded by his Father's faith

He saw and tasted the fruits revealed
   by exotic lands

He laughed, he sang. His Spirit spoke:
   all share the same joy, the same sadness, the same hope

His journey would not lead him back to where
   the boy left to become a man

Another place would call where he would
   find true joy; but,

He knows when his days are done and all is left to God,
   he wants his Father's Delta earth to claim him for its own